# THE HEALTHY GOURMET INTERNATIONAL COOKBOOK

*Also by Barbara Bassett*

The Healthy Gourmet Cookbook

# THE HEALTHY GOURMET INTERNATIONAL COOKBOOK
## BARBARA BASSETT

## GREAT NATURAL RECIPES
## FROM AROUND THE WORLD

*Arlington Books*
*King Street St. James's*
*London*

THE HEALTHY GOURMET INTERNATIONAL COOKBOOK
*First published 1985 by*
*Arlington Books (Publishers) Ltd*
*London S.W.1*

© *1985 Barbara Bassett*

*Typeset by Inforum Ltd, Portsmouth*
*Printed and bound by*
*The Guernsey Press, Guernsey*

*British Library Cataloguing in Publication Data*
*Bassett, Barbara*
*The healthy gourmet international cookbook.*
*1. Cookery*
*I. Title*
*641.5        TX717*

*ISBN 0–85140–663–7*

*For Norman*

# Contents

| | |
|---|---:|
| Introduction | 1 |
| Appetizers and Snacks | 5 |
| Soups | 14 |
| Salads & Salad Dressings | 37 |
| Mustard | 49 |
| Cheese & Egg Main Courses | 55 |
| Fish | 67 |
| Chicken & other Poultry | 75 |
| Meats | 94 |
| Beans, Grains & Pasta | 119 |
| Rice | 135 |
| Vegetables | 143 |
| Breads & Pastries | 163 |
| Cakes & Sweets | 170 |
| Pressure Cooking | 181 |
| Glossary | 184 |
| Weights and Measures | 190 |
| Index | 191 |

# Introduction
## Experiments & Adventures

Working with the good natural gifts of the earth, treating them with reverence and respect, combining flavours and textures for harmony and contrast, and creating a dish that is both nutritious and appealing is the essence of fine cooking. The good cook takes the finest natural ingredients and prepares them to bring out their essential character, flavour, aroma, texture and colour. The *great* cook, while retaining all those elements, invents subtle variations which obliterate boredom, even with very simple fare.

Adventurousness is the key, but tempered by knowledge and experience. While willingness to explore has definite cultural boundaries, I suspect that another boundary is determined by immediate environment, eg: Mum's cooking. Almost without exception, people whose parents were incompetent or indifferent cooks are not particularly interested in broadening their culinary horizons. While all of us find comfort from time to time in the simple foods of childhood, a growth of the sensibilities of taste should accompany the rest of growth. My grandmother made a delicious, dense, deep-yellow "white" bread which I adored as a child. However, before I reached my teens, my nutrition-oriented mother was fervently supporting wholegrain bread. Now, while I recall my grandmother's bread with fondness, I find white bread (even homemade) appallingly dull.

Although most of experimentation involves a small step from the well-known to the less-familiar (spinach instead of lettuce/bulghur instead of potatoes/yogurt instead of sour cream, *et cetera*), the interested chef will soon uncover a whole new realm of "exotic" foods and condiments. In truth, what is exotic about these items is simply that they are new and unfamiliar or used in unusual ways. For example, Vegetable Couscous is simply a vegetable stew made with a grain (couscous) whose name may be unfamiliar, but whose flavour and texture are comfortingly similar to pasta. What makes this stew "exotic" is the combination of vegetables juxtaposed with cinnamon and cayenne. Furthermore, by varying the vegetables to suit season, taste and purse, and adjusting the spices to individual preference, Couscous offers itself to limitless variation. Couscous can also be made with chicken or lamb or both. *More* variations.

Most of the world's consistently popular dishes are not particularly elaborate. They can be prepared at home with a minimum of fuss, and have a wide appeal.

Some years ago, Beef Wellington made a sort of social splash as the "in" thing to serve at a dinner party. It had previously been a dish available only in exclusive restaurants. For a few dreadful years, nearly every hostess would serve up a "Wellington" of some description, unremarkable at best. While it is entirely possible for an experienced, dedicated cook to make a Beef Wellington at home, it's still not an everyday affair. As a footnote, rather shabby "Beef Wellington" appears on the menus of restaurants who should know better.

On the other hand, **Sauce Bolognese** (tomato sauce with meat) is served in millions of homes and in infinite variation. Rarely do two cooks make it quite the same way — or make it the same way twice — and it's almost *always* good. Whatever ingredients are used, which herbs, whether the tomatoes are chopped or puréd, the *one* ingredient which will destroy a Bolognese (or any other tomato sauce) is sugar, honey or any other sweetener. Other than that, Sauce Bolognese is an improviser's delight. You *can* go too far, though; we've been served Bolognese with chopped cranberries. Yes, it *was* awful!

Part of the appeal of good food, well served, is the way it *looks*. When you start with ingredients that are intrinsically attractive, the rest is easy. Who can resist the delicate coral-pink of **Dublin Bay Prawns**, sprinkled with fresh green parsley and crowned with lemon wedges? The ruby sparkle of **Borscht** will brighten any appetite, and the subtle contrast of plump, juicy green grapes and moist flaky sole have made **Sole Véronique** a classic.

As you experiment, keep in mind that a recipe is simply someone else's formula for concocting a specific dish. *Your* "formula" may be quite different, depending on how much or little *you* like salt, sugar, pepper, garlic, oregano — what have you. But please, *never* dismiss an ingredient after just one try.

The first time I was served a *raita* of cucumber and yogurt with fresh coriander, I thought the coriander tasted a lot like soap. After encountering it again and again in many different Asian and Central American foods, I treasure the stuff, and am uncomfortable when cooking one of these delightful dishes without it. Another time, a dear friend "hated" aubergine until I buried it in a creamy, savoury moussaka. That was more than acceptable. Not wishing to belabour the point, I kept silent when one of several appetizer courses served in a restaurant appeared to be aubergine in yogurt and garlic sauce. It was. My friend enjoyed it.

Just as your mood, energy and appetite change from day to day, your taste changes. Say "no," say "not now," but *don't* say "never." Experiment and enjoy.

# Appetizers

## Baba Ghannouj (Mid-East)

Sometimes called "poor man's caviar," Baba Ghannouj is much too good to be labelled "poor man's" anything. Serve as a dip or with crisp biscuits.

1 *medium aubergine*
1 *tablespoon tahini*
$\frac{1}{4}$ *cup lemon juice*
2 *cloves garlic, minced very fine*

$\frac{1}{2}$ *teaspoon kelp*
*cayenne to taste*
$\frac{1}{4}$ *cup chopped parsley*

1. Grill the aubergine until the skin is blackened, or toast over a gas flame.
2. Let cool. Peel away the skin. Mash the pulp until creamy, but not perfectly smooth.
3. Mix together the tahini, lemon juice, garlic, kelp and cayenne. Beat into the aubergine. Heap into a bowl and chill. Serve sprinkled with parsley.

## Caponata (Italian)

A savoury mixture of vegetables with a distinctly Mediterranean flavour, Caponata is served cold, in very small portions.

1 *aubergine, about 1$\frac{1}{4}$ lb.*
*salt*
2 *tablespoons olive oil*
2 *cloves garlic, peeled and cracked*

1 *cup finely chopped celery*
$\frac{1}{2}$ *cup finely chopped onion*
5 *medium tomatoes, peeled, seeded and chopped (1 lb. tin drained)*

¼ *cup red wine vinegar mixed*        8  *green olives, stoned and*
   *with* 1 *teaspoon honey*            *sliced*
*pepper*                             1  *tablespoon capers, rinsed*
                                   *twice.*

1. Cut unpeeled aubergine into 1″ cubes. Sprinkle with salt and place in colander for 1 hour. Rinse and pat dry.
2. Heat oil. Sauté garlic until it is lightly browned. Discard garlic.
3. Add the celery and onion to the pan and sauté until onion is limp. Add tomatoes and aubergine. Stir to coat with oil. Add vinegar, honey and a light sprinkle of pepper. Stir.
4. Cover pan and allow mixture to steam over medium heat about 20 minutes or until aubergine is soft, stirring occasionally.
5. Stir in the olives and capers. Cover and steam about 5 minutes more. Let cool. Chill.

**NOTE:** Caponata is best when it has been aged several days. It can also be frozen for up to six months.

## Marvellous Mushroom Paté (French)

2 *medium sized yellow onions*       2 *tablespoons tomato paste*
  *(12 oz.)*                          2 *tablespoons lemon juice*
1 *small red onion (3 oz.)*           1 *teaspoon paprika*
3 *cloves garlic*                     1  *teaspoon  Worcestershire*
1 *lb. fresh mushrooms*                 *sauce*
¼ *lb. butter*                        ¼ *teaspoon cayenne*

1. Mince the onions. Steam in a sieve above boiling water 10 minutes.
2. Mince the garlic and mushrooms. Add to the onions and steam 10 minutes more.
3. Combine the hot mushroom mixture with all remaining ingredients. Purée in a blender or food processor. The mixture should retain a little texture.

4. Pack into an attractive serving bowl, cover tightly and chill thoroughly.
   *Serves 8–10.* Recipe may be halved.
   Garnish with lemon and parsley.

## Dolmades

Greek stuffed grape leaves — deliciously different.

| | |
|---|---|
| 1 *jar grape leaves (1 lb.)* | 2 *tablespoons minced fresh* |
| 4 *fl. oz. oil* | *parsley* |
| 1 *onion, minced* | $\frac{1}{4}$ *cup lemon juice* |
| $\frac{1}{2}$ *lb. minced lamb or beef** | $\frac{1}{4}$ *lb. raw brown rice* |
| 2 *cloves garlic, crushed* | 8 *fl. oz. hot water* |
| 4 *spring onions, chopped finely* | $\frac{1}{4}$ *cup currants or chopped* |
| 2 *tablespoons minced fresh dill* | *raisins (optional)* |

*Soy granules, softened in water and drained, can be used instead of meat.

1. Place the grape leaves in a large colander and rinse them with hot water. Set aside.
2. Heat the olive oil in a large pot and sauté the onion until it is translucent. Add the lamb and stir until the lamb is crumbly. Add the garlic, spring onions, dill, parsley and lemon juice. Mix well.
3. Add the rice and stir until the rice is translucent. Add the hot water. Cover the pot and let simmer 10 minutes.
4. Remove from heat and stir in the currants. Let cool slightly.
5. Line the bottom of a large pot with some of the grape leaves. To stuff the leaves, place them shiny side down (veins up). Remove the stems. Place a portion of the filling at the stem end of each leaf. Roll toward the centre and fold in the sides of the leaf. Finish rolling. Place the rolled leaf, seam side down in the prepared pan. Continue until all the stuffing is used and place a few extra leaves to cover the stuffed leaves in the pan.

6. Add water to a depth of 1" below the top of the stuffed leaves. Place a saucer over the leaves and press it down gently. Cover the pot with a lid and simmer about 30 minutes or until the rice is done. Open a leaf to check.
7. Serve warm or at room temperature, topped with avgolemono sauce. (page    )
   *Serves 8–12 as an appetizer, 4 as a main dish.*

## Avgolemono Sauce (Greek)

Good on dolmades or any other vegetable dish.

½ *pint vegetable or chicken stock*
1 *tablespoon cornflour (or arrowroot)*

2 *fl. oz. lemon juice*
1 *egg, lightly beaten*

1. Heat the stock to boiling.
2. Mix together the cornflour and lemon juice until smooth. Beat into the egg. Beat in a little of the boiling stock.
3. Beat the egg mixture into the stock, off the heat.

## Humus Bi Tahini (Mid-East)

This is a spread made from mashed chick peas. It is good as a dip, and is wonderful on warm whole wheat toast.

1½ *cups cooked chickpeas*
4 *oz. sesame tahini*
3 *cloves garlic*

*juice of one lemon*
1 *teaspoon salt*

*cooking water drained from the chickpeas*

*parsley and lemon wedges for garnish*

*paprika*

1. Mash the chickpeas. Force the garlic through a press and mix it into the tahini, add the lemon juice and salt and mix well.
2. Grind the mashed chickpeas in a blender, a few at a time, adding a bit of the tahini mixture and as much of the cooking water as needed to blend. Blend in small batches or use a food processor. The humus should be thick, and not perfectly smooth.
3. Serve garnished with parsley and lemon wedges.

## Liver Paté (French)

This is a very rich paté with a marvellous flavour.

$1\frac{1}{2}$ *pints salted water*
1 *leafy stalk celery*
1 *tablespoon fresh parsley*
4 *peppercorns*
1 *lb. chicken livers*
*pinch cayenne pepper*
6 *oz. soft butter*

$\frac{1}{2}$ *teaspoon nutmeg*
$\frac{1}{2}$ *teaspoon dry mustard*
1 *small onion, minced*
1 *clove garlic, minced*
*salt to taste*
2 *tablespoons very good brandy (optional)*

1. Bring the water to a boil. Add the celery, parsley and peppercorns. Add the livers and cook over low heat, covered, for about 10 minutes. Drain the livers, and chop them coarsely.
2. Mix the livers with all the remaining ingredients and process in a blender until smooth. Pack into small terrines and chill overnight. Use within three days.

## Pan Bagna (Italian)

A wonderful portable salad, pan bagna is equally at home in a picnic basket or as an elegant appetizer.

1 *large loaf of whole wheat French bread*
3 *tomatoes, peeled, seeded and chopped*
4 *spring onions, chopped*
½ *cup black olives, stoned and chopped*
½ *cup green olives, stoned and chopped*
2 *tablespoons chopped parsley*
1 *teaspoon capers*
1 *tablespoon grated Parmesan cheese*
2 *tablespoons olive oil*
2 *green peppers, seeded and chopped*
1 *sweet Spanish onion, finely chopped (optional)*
*lemon juice*

1. Cut the ends from the bread. Using a long spoon, hollow the loaf, reserving the crumbs.
2. Mix the breadcrumbs with the tomatoes, spring onions, olives, parsley, capers, cheese, oil, peppers and onion. Mix well. Moisten and season to taste with the lemon juice.
3. Stuff the breadcrumb and vegetable mixture into the hollow loaf. Wrap the loaf tightly and chill well.
4. To serve, unwrap the loaf and cut it into 1½″ thick slices. *Makes 8 portions.*


## Piroshki (Russian)

Serve these little cabbage-filled pastries alone, or as the traditional accompaniment to Borscht.

1 *recipe sour cream pastry (see page   )*
½ *small cabbage, shredded*
1 *small onion, finely chopped*
1 *tablespoon oil*
2 *hard-boiled eggs, finely chopped*
*salt and pepper to taste*
1 *egg, beaten*

1. Heat the oil in a large, heavy frying pan and toss the

cabbage and onion until well mixed. Cover the pan tightly and steam over low heat, stirring occasionally, for about 10 minutes. Let cool.

2. Mix the hard-boiled eggs into the cabbage and season highly with salt and ppper.

3. Roll the pastry on a floured board to $\frac{1}{4}''$ thick. Cut rounds 3 or 4 inches in diameter. Place a tablespoonful of the cabbage mixture in the centre of each round. Brush the edges with the beaten egg. Bring the edges together and seal. Set the piroshki on a greased baking sheet so that the fluted, sealed edge is uppermost.

4. Preheat oven to 400°F. Brush the piroshki with any remaining beaten egg and bake for about 15 minutes or until they are golden brown. Serve hot.

## Coconut Chips (Americas)

Here's a wholesome snack food that's really delicious.

| | |
|---|---|
| 1 *coconut* | 2 *teaspoons powdered kelp* |
| 1 *teaspoon medium paprika* | $\frac{1}{2}$ *teaspoon celery seed* |
| 1 *teaspoon garlic powder* | 1 *teaspoon salt* |
| $\frac{1}{8}$ *teaspoon cayenne* | |

1. Puncture the eyes of the coconut and drain liquid (save for cooking). Place the coconut in a 325°F. oven for 20 minutes.

2. Remove and tap with a hammer to crack. Remove the shell and peel away the brown skin. Pare the coconut meat into thin chips. Place the chips on a baking sheet and bake at 350°F. for 10 minutes, stirring once.

3. Place the chips in a large bowl. Mix the spices together and add to the chips. Toss to mix well.

4. Return the chips to the oven as before and bake 10 minutes more, stirring once or twice. If they are browning too fast, remove from the oven. Allow to cool.

5. Store in glass jars, refrigerated, for up to two weeks, or freeze.

6. To use: Heat chips on baking sheet in 250°F. oven until warm.

## Pitta with Herbs (Mid-East)

Really a do-it-yourself sandwich, it can also be a first course or a light lunch.

4 *whole pitta bread, warmed*
¼ *lb. feta cheese*
Any or all of the following
     to taste:

| | |
|---|---|
| *radishes* | *sprouts* |
| *spring onions* | *watercress* |
| *parsley* | *fresh mint* |
| *cilantro (coriander) leaves* | *fresh tarragon* |

1. Arrange pitta and vegetables on a platter.
2. To serve: Tear or cut pitta in half to form two hemispheres. Sprinkle a little feta into the pocket and top with vegetables to taste.
   *Serves 4.*


## Cherry Syrup for Beverages (Mid-East)

When cherries are in season, make this syrup for a refreshing drink.

1 *lb. stoned cherries (as sour as possible)*
1 *pint water*
2 *tablespoons honey*
1 *tablespoon strained lemon or lime juice*
1 *tablespoon agar-agar flakes*

1. Add the cherries to the water and bring to a boil. Simmer 15 minutes.
2. Place a cheesecloth-lined colander over a bowl. Pour the cherries and their liquid into the colander and let drain 30 minutes. Discard the cherries. There will be about 1 cup of liquid.
3. Add the honey and lemon or lime juice to the cherry liquid. Adjust sweetness to taste, if desired. Stir in the agar flakes. Let rest 10 minutes. Stir.

4. Bring the mixture to a boil. Cook over moderate heat 10 minutes. Do not stir, but skim away foam if needed. Cool.
5. Pour mixture into glass jar when cool. Refrigerate, tightly covered.

TO USE: Mix 2 to 3 tablespoons cherry syrup with 1 glass of water. Pour over ice for a refreshing drink.

# Soups

### Jerusalem Artichoke Soup (Americas)

Despite the name, Jerusalem artichokes (sunchokes) are native North Americans.

1 lb. Jerusalem artichokes, peeled and sliced
1 large onion, chopped
2 leafy stalks celery, chopped
1½ pints water
1 teaspoon dill seed
½ cup packed fresh sorrel leaves (optional)
2 tbs. lemon juice

1. Put everything except the lemon juice into a large pan. Bring to a boil. Lower heat, cover and simmer 25 minutes.
2. Let soup cool. Purée in a blender or food processor. Add lemon juice to taste. Serve hot or cold.
   Serves 4.

### Balkan Christmas Soup

Simple, different and delicious, Balkan Christmas Soup is made from ingredients readily available in the midst of winter.

3 oz. European-style dried mushrooms
12 oz. sauerkraut juice
1½ pints water
½ oz. butter
1 small onion, finely chopped
1 oz. whole-wheat flour
salt and pepper to taste
peeled, boiled potatoes

1. Soak the mushrooms in warm water for about 30 minutes. Drain the mushrooms, reserving the liquid, and wash them very well. Rinse with warm water.

2. Mix together the water and sauerkraut juice and bring to a boil. Add the mushrooms and simmer $1\frac{1}{2}$ hours. Add enough water to make $2\frac{1}{2}$ pints. Keep at simmer.
3. Melt the butter in a frying pan and sauté the onion until golden. Stir in the flour. Stir in about 1 cup of the stock from the soup. Mix well and return the mixture to the soup. Add salt and pepper to taste.
4. To serve, place a few potatoes in each diner's bowl and ladle the soup over.
   *Serves 6 generously.*

## Caribbean Black Bean Soup

The black, or turtle, beans used to make this soup are probably native to Mexico. They have a rich, mellow flavour unlike any other bean and make a truly excellent soup.

1 *lb. black beans*
2 *tablespoons annatto oil\* (optional)*
1 *large onion, finely chopped*
2–3 *cloves garlic, chopped*
2 *tablespoons tomato paste*
2 *tablespoons cider vinegar*
1 *teaspoon ground cumin seed*
$\frac{1}{2}$ *teaspoon cayenne (or to taste)*
*salt to taste*
$\frac{1}{4}$ *cup fresh lime juice (lemon may be substituted)*
*fresh coriander leaves to garnish*

1. Place the beans in a large pot and cover with water until the water is 2 inches above the beans. Bring to a boil, cover and simmer 2–3 hours or until soft.
2. Allow to cool. Drain and reserve the liquid. Measure the liquid and add stock or water to make $2\frac{1}{2}$ pints. Mash the beans OR purée the beans with their liquid in a blender, a little at a time OR process the beans with a little liquid in a food processor, about one third at a time. In any case, you should have a nice, thick mixture with a slightly grainy texture.
3. Heat the annatto oil and sauté the onion and garlic

*See Glossary

until very limp, but not brown. Stir this mixture into the beans (in a large pot).

4. Add the tomato paste, vinegar, cumin, cayenne and salt to taste. Heat to boiling, mixing very well. Remove from heat and stir in lime juice. Serve with a sprig of coriander on top.
*Makes 6–8 servings.*

## Borscht I (Russia)

Borscht, Russian beetroot soup, can be served hot or cold. Made with meat or meatless, the vegetables in borscht can be varied to taste — only the beetroot is indispensable.

THE STOCK
1½ *lb. beef short ribs*
2 *quarts water*
1 *onion, cut up,* not *peeled*
1 *carrot, in chunks*
¼ *cup cider vinegar*

THE SOUR
3 or 4 *med. beetroot (10 oz.) peeled and diced*
1 *leek, diced*
1 *carrot, diced*
4 *tomatoes, peeled, seeded and chopped*
1 *cup chopped cabbage*
¼ *teaspoon lemon peel*

SEASONINGS
*salt, pepper and lemon juice to taste*

GARNISH
*sour cream or yogurt*
*minced dill weed*

1. Place all ingredients for stock in a large pot and simmer 4 hours or until meat is tender, OR cook 12 hours in a slow-cooker.
2. Chill the stock thoroughly and remove all traces of fat. Strain stock.
3. Remove the meat from bones. Discard any fat. Dice the meat and return to the strained stock.
4. Bring stock to a boil and add the vegetables for the

soup. Cook on medium heat 40 minutes or until beet-root is tender. Season to taste.
5. Serve with a dollop of sour cream or yogurt and a sprinkling of dill.
Good hot or cold.
*Serves 6.*

## Borscht II(Russia)

4 to 5 *medium beetroot (about* ¾ *lb.)*
*beetroot greens*
4 *cloves garlic*
1 *large onion, in chunks*
1 *large tomato, in chunks*
2 *medium carrots, in chunks*
3 *pints water*
½ *small head cabbage, shredded*
*juice of one lemon*
*salt and white pepper to taste*
*plain yogurt*

1. Scrub the beetroot well, but do not peel them. Pick the best of the beetroot greens and wash them well.
2. Place the beetroot, greens, garlic, onion, tomato, carrots and water in a large pot. Bring to a boil and simmer for 1½ hours.
3. Remove the vegetables from the broth and purée them. Return to the broth and stir in the cabbage and lemon juice. Simmer for 10 minutes and season to taste. Serve hot with a generous dollop of yogurt.
Serve hot or cold.
*Serves 6, generously.*

## Bouillabaise (French)

The supreme fish soup. It should be made with any fish available, the more variety, the better.

2–3 *lbs. mixed fish*
2 *dozen mussels and/or clams,*
   *if available*
½ *lb. fresh prawns*
2 *tablespoons olive oil*
2 *tablespoons safflower oil*
2 *leeks, washed carefully and*
   *chopped   coarsely   (white*
   *part only)*
2 *large onions, chopped coarse-*
*ly*

3 *cloves garlic, minced*
2 *cups home-bottled tomatoes*
*Bouquet garni (thyme, bay*
   *leaf, parsley, celery leaf tied*
   *together)*
*pinch  saffron  in  ½  cup  dry*
   *sherry*
¼ *teaspoon grated orange peel*
*salt and pepper to taste*

1. Cut fish into chunks about 2″ by 2″. Save heads and any extra bones and skin to make stock. Eel should be cut into pieces about 3″ long. Strong fish, such as haddock, cod, eel, mackerel and sea bass should be separated from more delicate fish such plaice, sole, red or grey mullet, rainbow trout or sea perch. Refrigerate fish until time to cook.
2. Make a stock from the heads and bones following the recipe for fish stock.* You will, of course, have less than two lbs. of fish to make the stock but you will have plenty of fish in the soup for extra flavour.
3. Scrub clams thoroughly and keep under cold water until ready to use. Scrub mussels and remove beards. Keep under cold water until time to cook.
4. Shell and devein prawns and chill.
5. Heat oils together in a large pot. Add leeks, onions, garlic and tomatoes. Cook a few minutes or until onions are becoming limp. Add strong fish and the *bouquet garni.* Cook over gentle heat about seven minutes. Add the saffron sherry, orange peel, delicate fish, fish stock to cover and salt and pepper to taste.

* See page 36.

Bring to a boil, simmer 15 minutes. Add prawns, clams and mussels. Cook until all shells open. (If one is rather stubborn, throw it out!) Discard the *bouquet garni* and ladle the Bouillabaise into large bowls.
*Serves 8.*


## Carrot Soup (Americas)

Simple ingredients are combined with subtle seasonings in an excellent carrot soup.

| | |
|---|---|
| 2 *tablespoons vegetable oil* | 2 *oz. raw brown rice* |
| 1 *medium onion, chopped* | *dash cinnamon* |
| 1 *lb. finely chopped carrots (or grated)* | ¼ *cup fresh lemon juice* |
| | *salt and white pepper to taste* |
| 1¼ *pints water or stock* | 1 *cup plain yogurt* |
| 2 *tablespoons tomato paste* | *chopped fresh parsley to garnish* |

1. Heat the oil and sauté the onion until just translucent. Stir in the carrots, water or stock, tomato paste and rice. Bring to a boil, cover and simmer 45 minutes.*
2. Add the cinnamon, lemon juice and salt and pepper to taste. Stir in the yogurt. Heat through. Garnish.
   *Makes 4 –6 servings.*

* If a smoother soup is desired, puree the soup in a processor or blender at this point.


## Cream of Chestnut Soup (Americas)

Cream of Chestnut Soup is a modern adaptation of a Colonial recipe. Since chestnuts are so much trouble to skin, I like to double or treble the recipe and freeze it.

| | |
|---|---|
| 1½ *lbs. fresh chestnuts, skinned* | 2 *leafy stalks celery, chopped* |
| 1½ *pints chicken stock* | 1 *cup milk (about)* |
| 2 *oz. butter* | *salt and cayenne pepper to taste* |
| 2 *medium onions, chopped* | |

1. Place chestnuts in large pot and just cover with stock. (Set remaining stock aside). Add 1 oz. butter. Bring to a boil, cover and simmer 30 minutes.
2. Heat the remaining butter and sauté the onion and celery until soft. Add the rest of the stock, cover and simmer 10 minutes. Strain the stock and discard the vegetables.
3. Purée the cooked chestnuts in a blender or sieve, adding the stock as needed. Mix the chestnut purée with any leftover stock and enough milk to make a thick, creamy soup. Season to taste.
*Serves 4.*


## Herbed Chickpea Soup (Mid-East)

Chickpeas combine with lentils, barley and lamb (or beef) in this robust soup with a generous helping of herbs.

| | |
|---|---|
| 2 *cups cooked chickpeas* | 3 *oz. pearl barley* |
| 1½ *pints rich lamb broth** | 1 *clove garlic, minced* |
| 3 *oz. brown lentils* | 1 *cup cooked lamb in* ½" *dice* |

HERB MIXTURE

| | |
|---|---|
| ½ *cup chopped parsley* | ½ *cup chopped spring onions* |
| 2 *tablespoons chopped corian-der leaves* | ½ *cup chopped sorrel or cress or spinach* |

GARNISH

| | |
|---|---|
| 1 *large onion, halved and sliced* | 1 *teaspoon turmeric* |
| 1 *tablespoon oil or clarified butter* | 1 *teaspoon dried mint* |

\* For **Meatless Version** substitute vegetable broth and omit lamb.

1. Cook chickpeas, broth, lentils, barley and garlic at a low simmer, covered for 40 minutes. Have herb mixture ready.
2. Add lamb and herb mixture to chickpeas. Stir well. Cover and simmer 15 minutes more.

3. Meanwhile, heat the oil or butter and cook the onion over moderate heat until golden brown. Add the turmeric. Lower heat and stir until onion is crisp (but not burnt). Mix in the mint.
4. Taste the soup for seasoning and add salt and pepper to taste. Add half the onion mixture. Garnish with the rest.
*Serves 4.*
NOTE: Beef and beef stock may be substituted.

## Belgian Chicken Soup (Waterzooi)

Rich and velvety, this delightful soup is thickened with a vegetable purée. If you can find a tasty old hen it will take longer to cook, but the taste is worth it.

| | |
|---|---|
| 1 *chicken, 3–5 lbs., cut up* | $\frac{1}{2}$ *teaspoon pepper* |
| *giblets (if any)* | 1 *bay leaf* |
| 3 *pints water* | $\frac{1}{2}$ *teaspoon dried thyme* |
| 2 *large onions, chopped* | 1 *clove* |
| 2 *leafy stalks celery, chopped* | *few leaves parsley* |
| 2 *medium carrots, chopped* | $\frac{1}{2}$ *cup white wine (optional)* |
| 1 *teaspoon salt* | 1 *cup plain yogurt or double cream* |

1. Place the chicken, giblets (if any), water, onions, celery, carrots, salt and pepper in a pot. Combine the bay leaf, thyme, clove and parsley in a small bag or herb ball and add to the pot. Bring to a boil. Skim off scum and foam as it rises.
2. RANGETOP: Cover pot loosely and simmer soup 1–1$\frac{1}{2}$ hours.
PRESSURE COOKER: Cover, bring to pressure, cook 20 minutes. Reduce pressure quickly.
3. Strain the broth. Discard the herbs, chicken skin and bones. Dice the chicken meat and giblets and return to the broth. Purée the vegetables, or mash them through a sieve and return to the broth.
4. Heat the broth to boiling. Stir in the wine.

5. Off heat, stir in the yogurt or cream. Serve hot.
    NOTE: If you like a thicker soup, stir in arrowroot paste
(p. 185) in step 4.
    *Serves 8.*


## Jellied Consommé Citron (Americas)

What a wonderful way to begin a summer meal!

¾ *pint good-flavoured chicken*      1   *cup fresh orange juice,*
    *stock, degreased\**                         *strained\**
1 *packet plain gelatine*             2   *tablespoons fresh lime or*
1 *egg white, beaten until just*          *lemon juice, strained*
    *foamy*                            2   *tablespoons Madeira or*
                                          *Sherry (optional)*

1. Place the stock in a large saucepan (about 5 pints).
   Sprinkle the gelatine on top and let stand 5 minutes.
2. Add the egg white to the stock and bring quickly to a
   boil while stirring with a wire whisk.
3. When the foam rises, remove the pan from heat and let
   stand 5 minutes without stirring.
4. Line a large strainer or colander with a tea towel. Set
   the strainer over a large bowl and pour the stock, foam
   and all, onto the tea towel, allowing the stock to strain
   through without stirring or squeezing. Gently lift away
   the tea towel and foam.
5. Add remaining ingredients to the clarified stock. Stir
   well. Chill at least 8 hours before serving. Garnish with
   a mint leaf or thin slice of lemon.
   *Serves 4.*

\* The flavour of this delicate consommé depends on the quality of
both the chicken stock and the orange juice. Both should be strong
and rich.

## Quick Corn Chowder (Americas)

Here's an all-American chowder incorporating two native American vegetables, corn and potatoes.

1 *tablespoon oil*
½ *medium onion, chopped finely*
2 *medium potatoes, diced, not peeled*
¾ *pint skimmed milk*
¼ *teaspoon thyme*

1 *tin whole-kernel sweet corn (16½ oz.), not drained*
2 *teaspoons cornflour mixed with 4 teaspoons water*
*salt and pepper to taste*

1. Heat the oil and sauté the onion until just translucent. Add the potatoes, milk and thyme and simmer, covered for 15 minutes.
2. Add the corn with its liquid and simmer 10 minutes more.
3. Stir in the cornflour mixture and season to taste with salt and pepper.
   *Makes 4–6 servings.*


## Israeli Fruit Soup

Once you've tried this wonderful soup, you'll think of countless variations — peaches, cherries, plums . . .

2 *cups berries*
2 *cups seedless grapes*
½ *melon, pared and seeded*
2 *large, tart apples, cored*
1½ *pints water*

4 *tablespoons lemon juice*
1 *stick cinnamon*
¼ *pint white wine (optional)*
*yogurt*

1. Place fruit, water, half of lemon juice and cinnamon stick in pot.
2. PRESSURE COOKER: Cover, bring to pressure, cook 4 minutes, cool immediately. Remove cinnamon stick.
   RANGETOP: Cover, cook at simmer 20 minutes. Remove cinnamon stick.

3. Purée the fruit mixture. Chill.
4. To serve, stir in wine and remaining lemon juice. Pass yogurt as a garnish.

NOTE: Fruit-flavoured liqueur is often added to the chilled soup as a flavouring.

*Serves 6.*

## Gazpacho (Spanish)

Gazpacho is the salad you drink. Use the best quality vinegar and oil, and let the flavours marry overnight.

1 *small onion, chopped*
1 *pepper, as ripe as possible, chopped (not seeded)*
1 *large cucumber, chopped (reserve a few slices for garnish)*
3 *ripe tomatoes, about 1½ lbs., peeled\* and chopped*
1 *or 2 cloves garlic, chopped*
¼ *cup cider vinegar*
2 *teaspoons sweet paprika*
2 *tablespoons olive oil (or other vegetable oil)*

1. Assemble all the vegetables in a large bowl. Blend to a smooth purée a little at a time, blending in the vinegar, paprika and oil.
2. Place the purée in a glass or ceramic bowl, and mix very well. Chill.
3. Garnish with the cucumber slices and serve cold.

NOTE: Gazpacho is best when made a day in advance.

\* Peel ripe tomatoes by dropping them in boiling water for 10 seconds. Drain. Rinse. Remove stem end and slip off the skin.

## Gulyas Soup (Hungarian)

The marvellous flavour of real Hungarian Goulash (*Gulyas*) is captured in this spicy soup, which may be garnished with the simple egg dumplings called *csipetke*.

1 *oz. butter*
2 *medium onions, chopped*
1 *tablespoon hot paprika*
1½ *lbs. beef in ½" cubes*

½ *medium-sized raw potato,*
  *grated*
1 *tablespoon tomato paste*
3 *pints beef or vegetable stock*

½ *teaspoon caraway seeds*
2 *lb. potatoes, diced*
1 *sweet green pepper, diced*
*salt to taste*

1. Heat the butter and sauté the onion until soft.
2. Add the paprika, beef and grated potato. Cover and simmer over low heat for 10 minutes.
3. Add 1 cup of stock, stir in the tomato paste, cover and simmer until meat is tender (usually about 25 minutes).
4. Add the remaining stock and bring to a boil. Add the caraway seeds, diced potato and pepper and simmer until the potato is tender. Salt to taste. Serve with Csipetke.
*Serves 6.*

## Csipetke (Tiny dumplings)

3 *oz. whole-wheat flour*
1 *egg*
*pinch salt*

Mound the flour on a bread board. Make a well in the centre. Sprinkle the salt on the flour. Break the egg into the well, and mix into the flour with a fork. Knead mixture thoroughly and break bean-size pieces into the simmering soup. Let simmer 10 minutes.

## Italian Lentil Soup

Here's a lovely, hearty soup that's so easy it almost cooks itself, and so good that the whole family will love it.

6 *oz. lentils*
1 *chopped carrot*
1 *stalk celery with leaves, chopped*
2 *small, finely diced onions*
2 *peeled, seeded, chopped tomatoes*
1 *tablespoon diced bacon or smoked sausage (optional)*

2 *cloves garlic, crushed or minced*
¼ *teaspoon dried oregano (1 teaspoon fresh)*
1½ *pints water*
*salt and pepper to taste*
*chopped parsley*
*grated Parmesan cheese*

Put everything except the parsley and cheese into a large, heavy pan. Simmer gently for 1½ hours. Stir occasionally. If the soup gets too thick, add a little more water. Serve hot, sprinkled with parsley and cheese.
*Serves at least four.*

## Lentil and Chard Soup (North Africa)

Easy, economical, delicious *and* good hot or cold.

6 *oz. brown lentils*
2 *pints water*
2 *medium onions, chopped*
½ *teaspoon turmeric*
3 *cloves garlic, minced*

1 *lb. Swiss chard, shredded*
*juice of 2 lemons*
4 *medium tomatoes, peeled, seeded and chopped*
2 *tablespoons soy sauce*

1. Wash lentils in cool water. Place in a large pan with the water. Bring to a boil. Cover and simmer over low heat until tender, about 45 minutes.
2. Add all the remaining ingredients to the lentils. Simmer about 10 minutes, or until greens and onions are tender.
3. Serve hot or cold. This soup is best on the second day. *Serves 6.*

## Betty's Menudo (Americas)

Menudo is best if prepared a day or so in advance. Also, the timing is so uncritical that I like to simmer the tripe and water overnight in a slow cooker, add the remaining ingredients and let it simmer all day.

1½ *lbs. cleaned honeycomb tripe*    1 *medium onion, diced*
   *(beef or pork)*    1 *tablespoon dried oregano*
2 *pints water (add more if*    ¼ *cup fresh coriander leaves*
   *needed)*      *(cilantro) chopped*
10 *oz chili sauce (mild* or *hot)*    1 *tin chick peas, drained*

1. Rub tripe with salt. Rinse with cold water. Rub tripe with vinegar, rinse with cold water. Remove all fat. Cut tripe into pieces about ½″ square.
2. Add the tripe to the water, bring to a boil. Skim fat as it rises. Simmer slowly, 3–4 hours.
3. Add all remaining ingredients. Simmer at least 2 more hours. Tripe should be very tender.
4. Serve hot, with warm corn tortillas*, and sprinkle garnishes to taste on the soup.

MENUDO GARNISHES
*Finely diced onion*        *lemon juice (lemon wedges)*
*chopped fresh coriander leaves*

* Available tinned at most large supermarkets.

## Minestrone (Italian)

Italy's wonderful bean and vegetable soup.

4½ oz. (dry weight) dried haricot beans, soaked overnight
1½ pints water
2 medium onions, chopped
1 leek, sliced
2 carrots, sliced
1 leafy stalk celery, sliced
3 cloves garlic, chopped
3 tablespoons tomato paste
1 bay leaf
1 cup chopped cabbage
1 cup cut-up green beans
½ lb. Swiss chard leaves, chopped
2 tablespoons brewer's yeast
  (optional)
2 tablespoons soy sauce
1 teaspoon chopped basil leaves
1 tablespoon parsley, chopped
  finely
½ cup uncooked pasta (broken
  wholewheat spaghetti, for
  instance)
salt and pepper to taste

1.  In a large pan, combine the beans, water, onions, leek, carrots, celery, garlic, tomato paste and bay leaf. Bring to a boil, cover and simmer 1 hour or until beans are tender.
2.  Remove the bay leaf and add the cabbage, beans, chard, brewer's yeast, soy sauce, basil and parsley. Return to a boil and sprinkle in the pasta. Cook 20 minutes or until pasta is done. Season to taste.
3.  Freshly grated Parmesan cheese may be served to sprinkle on the soup.
    *Serves 6.*


## Onion Soup, Parisian Style

Authentic French onion soup is a deep golden colour with an unmistakable, *mild* onion flavour. It's also *very* easy to make.

FOR EACH PERSON
1 large onion, thinly sliced
1 tablespoon vegetable oil
½ oz. whole-wheat flour
½ pint rich stock (beef is traditional)
salt to taste

1 *or* 2 *slices day-old whole-*
*wheat French bread*
$\frac{1}{2}$ *oz. butter*

2 *tablespoons freshly grated*
*Parmesan cheese*

1. Sauté the onion in oil until translucent and soft, but *not* brown. Stir in the flour to mix well. Stir in the stock. Bring to a boil. Cover and simmer over low heat 25 minutes. Taste and add salt if necessary, but remember the cheese is salty!
2. Butter the bread and sprinkle with the cheese.
3. Place hot soup in an oven-proof bowl. Top with the bread (cheese side up) and place under a grill until cheese is bubbly.

NOTE: This recipe is for one person and can be increased to serve as many as you like. For several persons, the soup may be served in a single large bowl or tureen.

## Dutch Pea Soup

12 *oz. dried green split peas*
$\frac{1}{3}$ *lb. smoked pork hock (option-*
*al)*
$2\frac{1}{2}$ *pints water*
$\frac{1}{4}$ *cup chopped parsley*
1 *medium onion, chopped fine*
1 *leafy stalk celery, chopped*
*fine*

2 *cloves garlic, chopped*
$\frac{1}{4}$ *cup white wine*
4 *cloves*
$\frac{1}{2}$ *teaspoon dried thyme*
1 *teaspoon white peppercorns*
$\frac{1}{4}$ *cup chopped parsley*
*salt and/or kelp to taste*

1. Place peas, smoked hock, parsley, onion, celery, garlic and wine in a large pan. Tuck the cloves, thyme and peppercorns into a herb ball* or mesh bag and add to the peas. Bring to a boil, cover and simmer 1 hour.

* A herb ball is like a large tea ball. The purpose is to allow the herbs and spices to be easily removed from a finished dish. Cloves, in particular can overpower other flavours, especially when the food is frozen. Lacking a herb ball, a cheesecloth bundle tied with string works just fine.

2. Remove the hock, trim the meat and return the meat to the pot. Remove the herb ball.
3. Add salt and/or kelp to taste.
   *Serves 4.*
   Reheats well, but may thicken on standing. Add water if needed.

## Mexican Rice Soup

Leftover, cooked brown rice makes this tasty soup quick to prepare.

2 *cups cooked brown rice*
2 *cloves garlic, chopped*
½ *small onion, chopped*
1 *small ripe tomato, diced*
½ *red pepper, diced*
¼ *pint tomato sauce*
2 *tablespoons bran (optional)*

1½ *pints water or stock (or combination)*
1 *teaspoon powdered cumin*
2 *teaspoons chopped fresh oregano (1 teaspoon dried)*
2 *tablespoons chopped fresh coriander leaves (optional)*
*salt and pepper to taste*

Place the rice in a large pan with the garlic, onion, tomato, pepper, tomato sauce, bran, stock, cumin and oregano. Bring to a boil and let simmer 10 minutes. Stir in the coriander leaves and simmer 2 minutes more. Season with salt and pepper to taste. Serve hot. Add water if needed.
   *Makes 4 servings.*

## Soupe au Pistou (French)

Pistou is a garlicky Provençal version of *pesto* which transforms a very good vegetable soup into a super-terrific vegetable soup.

3½ *pints boiling, salted water*
2 *leeks, chopped*
1 *medium onion, sliced*
2 *medium carrots, sliced*

2 *tomatoes, peeled, seeded and chopped*
1 *potato, diced*
1 *turnip, diced*

2 cups pumpkin (or pumpkin-type squash) peeled and diced
3 cups cooked haricot beans
1 leafy stalk celery, chopped
1 bay leaf
3–4 sprigs parsley
pinch thyme
1 cup fresh or frozen string beans
2 courgettes sliced
1 cup whole-wheat elbow macaroni
salt and pepper to taste

1. In a large pan, combine the water, leeks, onion, carrots, tomatoes, potato, turnip, pumpkin, beans, celery, bay leaf, parsley and thyme. Cover and simmer 20 minutes.
2. Add beans, courgettes and macaroni and cook until macaroni is done. Season lightly.
   *Serves 6–8.*
   Serve in individual bowls or tureen. Pass *Pistou* separately.

## Pistou

4 large cloves garlic, peeled
¼ cup packed fresh basil leaves
2 oz. freshly grated Parmesan cheese
1 tablespoon broth from the soup
¼ pint olive oil (about)
salt and pepper to taste

1. Crush the garlic and basil in a mortar. Crushing with a pestle, mix a bit of cheese, a bit of broth, a bit of oil, mix alternately until a barely fluid paste is achieved. Season.
2. Serve the pistou in the mortar. Diners add a tablespoonful or two to their soup at the table.

## Provençal Farmhouse Soup

A main-dish soup with an intriguing flavour.

1 *tablespoon olive oil*
1 *medium onion, chopped*
2 *leeks, chopped*
4 *to 8 cloves garlic, minced*
4 *medium tomatoes, peeled, seeded & chopped**
2½ *pints water*
4 *medium potatoes, sliced about ¼" thick*
*Bouquet garni*

1 *piece dried orange peel, about 1" square*
*pinch fennel seed*
*pinch saffron*
*white pepper*
1½ *teaspoons salt*
6 *slices whole-wheat bread, preferably French*
6 *eggs*

1. Heat the oil in a large heavy pot. Stir in the onion, leeks and garlic until well coated with oil.
2. Add the tomatoes, water, potatoes, *bouquet garni*, orange peel, fennel and saffron. Bring to a boil and simmer, partly covered, for 20 minutes, or until the potatoes are done. Add the salt and pepper to taste. Remove the *bouquet garni* and orange peel and discard.
3. With a slotted spoon, remove the potatoes to a bowl and keep warm.
4. Add the eggs to the simmering broth one by one and poach five minutes, or until done to taste.
5. Place a slice of bread in the bottom of each soup bowl. Top with an egg and broth. Serve the potatoes on the side.
   *Serves 6.*

*1½ cups tinned tomatoes may be substituted.

## Scotch Broth

Very economical, Scotch Broth is a hearty lamb soup made thick and creamy by the addition of barley.

5 *pints water*
1 *teaspoon salt*

1½ *(or more) lbs. meaty lamb bones*

1 *tablespoon cider vinegar or*   2 *carrots*
*wine*   1 *cup barley*
2 *leeks (or one medium onion*   *salt and pepper to taste*
*plus* 2 *spring onions)*   *parsley to garnish*

1. Heat water to boiling. Add salt, bones and vinegar. Reduce heat, cover and simmer 1½ hours.
2. Mince leeks and carrots. Remove meat and bones from broth and let cool. Add leeks, carrots and barley to pan. Bring to a boil. Cover and simmer 45 minutes, or until barley is tender. Chop the meat and return it to the pan. Season to taste. Garnish.
*Serves 4 to 6.*
Freezes well.


## Stracciatella

This is the Italian version of egg drop soup, but the fresh Parmesan makes it very different.

2 *eggs*   *pinch grated nutmeg (option-*
2 *tablespoons whole-wheat*   *al)*
*flour*   2 *pints good-flavoured beef*
1½ *oz. freshly grated Parmesan*   *stock*
*cheese*

1. Mix together the eggs, flour, cheese, nutmeg, and a ladleful of cold stock. Set aside.
2. Heat the remaining stock to boiling. Whisk in the egg mixture and simmer 2 minutes. Serve hot.
*Serves 4.*

## Stroganoff Soup (Russian)

Elegant but very easy, this soup can be a whole meal when accompanied by a salad. It's a great way to use up a bit of leftover beef — or serve it meatless.

1½ oz. butter
1 medium onion, thinly sliced
2 cups sliced mushrooms
1 oz. whole-wheat flour
¾ pint stock or water

1 tablespoon Dijon style mustard
½ cup cooked beef (optional)
salt and pepper to taste
4 tablespoons sour cream
sour cream to garnish

1. Melt the butter and sauté the onion and mushrooms until soft.
2. Stir in the flour and cook, stirring for a minute. Stir in the stock and the mustard. Simmer for about 10 minutes, stirring occasionally.
3. Add the beef, if desired. Add salt and pepper to taste — the soup should be slightly *under*salted.
4. Remove the soup from heat and stir in the 4 tablespoons sour cream. Serve immediately, garnished with a dollop of sour cream.
   *Serves 2.*

## Zuppa di Baccala

Baccala (salt cod) is a staple in southern France, Portugal, Spain and Italy. This delectable soup is Italian.

¾ lb. dried salt cod (baccala)
1 small onion, chopped
2 or 3 sprigs celery leaves
½ lemon
3 tablespoons vegetable oil
2 onions, chopped
2 cloves garlic, minced
1 stalk celery, chopped
1 teaspoon chopped parsley

3 tablespoons tomato paste
1 bay leaf
pinch thyme
8 fl. oz. dry white wine
1½ pints stock from cod or water
2 large potatoes, sliced
salt and pepper to taste

1. Place salt cod in a glass bowl, cover with water and let soak 18 to 24 hours, changing water every eight hours or so.
2. Cut cod into $\frac{1}{2}''$ pieces. Remove any skin or bones. Bring enough water to a boil to cover the cod. Add celery leaves, one small onion and half a lemon. Add cod, return to the boil. Boil one minutes, cover pot and set aside 10 minutes. Skim the broth and reserve. Remove and discard onion, celery and lemon.
3. Heat vegetable oil. Gently sauté the two onions, garlic and celery until the onion is translucent. Add parsley, tomato paste, bay leaf, thyme and wine and stir well. Pour in reserved broth from cod, adding enough water to make $1\frac{1}{2}$ pints. Stir in the potatoes and bring to a boil. Add cod. Let soup simmer for one hour, adding water if too thick. Taste for seasoning.
*Serves 6.*

## Chicken Stock

| | |
|---|---|
| *wingtips, neck, backbone and giblets from chicken* | *1 leafy celery stalk* |
| *1 onion* | *1 bay leaf* |
| | *1 teaspoon salt* |

1. Place everything in a large pot and add water to cover.
2. Bring to a boil, skimming as necessary.
3. Lower heat and simmer 30 minutes.
4. Strain and use for stock or soup. Use meat from bones in soup together with noodles or rice, carrots, celery, onions, peas, beans or whatever you like.
*Serves 4.*

## Fish Stock

2 *lbs. fish, including head and bones*

*shells and tails from shrimp and lobster, if available*

1 *onion, cut in chunks*

1 *carrot, cut in chunks*

1 *leafy celery stalk, cut in chunks*

1 *bay leaf*

½ *lemon, sliced*

*pinch salt*

¼ *pint white wine*

1. Put all ingredients in a large pan. Add water to cover generously.
2. Bring to a boil, skim, lower heat and simmer one and one half hours. Strain.

# Salads & Salad Dressings

## Caesar Salad (Americas)

From Caesar's in Tijuana to the world's finest restaurants — this salad is a favourite.

1 *clove garlic, crushed*
¼ *cup olive oil*
½ *cup safflower (or other) oil*
3 *slices whole-wheat bread*
2 *eggs*
1 *tin anchovies (optional)*

2 *medium-sized heads cos lettuce*
2 *tablespoons fresh lemon juice*
1 *oz. freshly grated Parmesan cheese*
*freshly ground pepper*

1. Add garlic to olive oil. Mix in safflower oil and let mixture stand overnight or at least 6 hours.
2. Trim crusts from bread and cut into ½-inch cubes. Sauté bread cubes in ¼ cup of garlic oil.
3. Boil eggs for one minute, chill immediately and keep chilled.
4. If you use anchovies, drain oil and rinse anchovies under warm water to make them less salty.
5. Wash and dry the lettuce. Tear leaves into large bowl.
6. Add remaining oil to the lettuce. Toss thoroughly. (At this point you can make a real production of the salad and bring all the ingredients to the table to finish.)
7. Break the eggs into the salad and toss to mix very well. Add lemon juice. Toss. Add the anchovies, bread cubes, cheese and pepper to taste. Toss with gusto. Serve with pride.

*Serves 4.*

## Greek Salad

Definitely a classic — its popularity is well-deserved.

SALAD
1 *small head cos lettuce (about*
   *8 oz.)*
1 *small head curly chicory (ab-*
   *out 8 oz.)*

2 *medium tomatoes, peeled &*
   *seeded*
4 *oz. feta cheese, cubed*
3 *spring onions, chopped*

DRESSING
¼ *pint oil*
⅛ *pint cider vinegar*

½ *teaspoon dried oregano (1*
   *teaspoon fresh)*

GARNISHES
½ *cup Greek olives (optional)*

1–2 *oz. tin anchovy fillets,*
   *drained & rinsed very well*
   *(optional)*

1. Wash the lettuce and chicory. Dry well and tear into
   bite size pieces. Chop the tomato coarsely. Toss all
   ingredients together.
2. Mix the dressing and pour over the salad. Toss well.
3. Add the garnishes, if desired.

## Salad Niçoise (French)

A wonderful combination of comestibles in a satisfying
main-course salad.

*vinaigrette dressing*
¾ *lb. string beans, sliced*
4–6 *oz. lettuce, washed and*
   *torn*
4 *tomatoes, peeled, seeded and*
   *sliced*
*French potato salad*

1 *small tin tuna, drained**
½ *cup stoned black olives, sliced*
   *(optional)*
2 *hard-boiled eggs, peeled and*
   *quartered*
2–3 *tablespoons finely chopped*
   *fresh herbs (optional)*

1. Steam the beans 15 minutes, or until tender-crisp. Toss
   with 2 tablespoons vinaigrette.

* Add or substitute sardines, if desired.

2. Toss the lettuce with 3 tablespoons vinaigrette and line a large bowl. Add the French potato salad. Arrange all remaining ingredients in order over the potato salad. Drizzle with remaining Vinaigrette.
*Serves 4.*

## Vinaigrette Dressing (French)

This is the real French Dressing!

| | |
|---|---|
| $\frac{1}{4}$ *pint vegetable oil* | $\frac{1}{2}$ *teaspoon Dijon mustard* |
| 2 *fl. oz. cider vinegar* | *(optional)* |

Mix all ingredients with a fork until thick and creamy.
*Makes about $\frac{1}{4}$ pint.*

## French Potato Salad

Seasoning the potatoes before they cool makes a world of difference.

| | |
|---|---|
| $1\frac{1}{2}$ *lb. potatoes, diced* | $\frac{1}{4}$ *cup Vinaigrette Dressing* |
| 1 *clove garlic, cracked* | $\frac{1}{4}$ *cup chopped fresh parsley* |
| $\frac{1}{4}$ *cup sherry or white wine* | $\frac{1}{8}$ *cup chopped red onion* |

Cook potatoes in boiling salted water 15 minutes. While potatoes cook, rub a large bowl well with garlic. Drain the potatoes, saving the water for stock. Place the drained potatoes in the garlic-rubbed bowl. Sprinkle on the sherry. Toss and let stand 20 minutes. Add Vinaigrette, parsley and onion. Toss well. Let cool. Chill until ready to serve.

## Mexican Christmas Salad

A beautiful melange of fruits and vegetables.

1 *banana, sliced*
1 *orange, peeled, seeded and diced*
1 *tart apple, cored and diced*
*juice of one lime (or lemon)*
8 *oz. washed, torn salad greens, preferably chicory and cos lettuce*

2 *beetroot, cooked, peeled and sliced*
1 *lime, peeled and sliced (lemon may be substituted)*
¼ *cup sunflower or pumpkin seeds*
1 *tablespoon cider vinegar*
¼ *pint safflower (or other) oil*

1. Toss the banana, orange and apple with the lime juice. Chill.
2. Place the greens in a large bowl. Arrange the beetroot atop the greens. Drain the fruit and arrange on the greens. Garnish with the peeled lime and sunflower seeds.
3. Mix together the drained juice from the fruit, the vinegar and the oil. Mix well and drizzle over the salad. *Serves 4.*

## Fruit Salad Delight (Americas)

¼ *cup lime or lemon juice*
1 *tablespoon ginger juice**
1 *banana*
½ *papaya (optional)*

¼ *melon*
1 *orange*
1 *satsuma (or another orange)*
1 *tablespoon sesame seeds*

1. Mix together the lime juice and ginger juice. Place in a large bowl.
2. Peel the banana and slice into the juice. Toss gently. Peel and seed the papaya, cut in chunks and add to the banana. Separate the melon flesh from the rind, cut the flesh into chunks and add to the papaya/banana mix-

* To make ginger juice, grate fresh ginger and squeeze the grated ginger through a cloth to extract the juice.

ture. Peel the orange and satsuma, separate the segments, remove any seeds and cut segments in half. Toss all the fruit together.

3. Chill 1–2 hours. Sprinkle with sesame seeds to serve. *Serves 4.*

## African Orange Salad

3–4 *navel oranges*
1  *cup thinly sliced fresh mushrooms*

DRESSING:

2 *tablespoons olive oil*
2 *cloves garlic, squished through a press*
½ *teaspoon paprika*

*dash cayenne*
½ *teaspoon lemon juice*
*pinch cumin powder*
2 *tablespoons chopped parsley*

Peel the oranges and section them. Use a sharp, serrated knife to remove *all* of the white membrane. Mix orange sections with the mushrooms. Chill. Mix together all of the ingredients for the dressing. Divide the orange-mushroom mixture into 4 serving plates and add ¼ of the dressing to each portion.

*Serves 4.*

## Waldorf Salad (Americas)

This is a lower-calorie version of an American favourite.

1½ *cups diced tart apple\**
¼ *cup lemon juice*

3 *medium stalks celery, diced*
3 *oz. coarsely chopped walnuts*

DRESSING

1 *tablespoon oil (preferably walnut)*
1 *tablespoon low-calorie mayonnaise*

2 *tablespoons plain yogurt*
*lettuce leaves*

\* 1 large apple, cored, unpeeled, yields 1½ cups.

1. Toss the diced apples with the lemon juice. Toss in the celery and walnuts.
2. Mix the dressing ingredients together and toss with the apple mixture.
3. Arrange lettuce leaves on serving dishes. Place a portion of salad on each dish.
   *Serves 6*

## Chicken Potato Salad (Mid-East)

The combination may be a bit unusual, but the result is delicious.

$\frac{1}{2}$ *lb. cooked, diced potatoes*
$\frac{1}{2}$ *lb. cooked, diced chicken*
1 *cup cooked peas*
$\frac{1}{4}$ *cup vinaigrette dressing (p. 39)*
$\frac{1}{4}$ *cup chopped sour pickles (optional)*
$\frac{1}{2}$ *cup yogurt*
*white pepper*
*lemon wedges*

1. Toss potatoes, chicken and peas with vinaigrette. Chill at least 1 hour.
2. Toss the chicken mixture with the pickles, yogurt and white pepper to taste. Serve with lemon wedges.
NOTE: If pickles are omitted, this recipe is salt-free.
   *Serves 4.*

## Herbed Chicken Salad (Americas)

Herbs and avocado make this chicken salad extraordinary.

2 *medium potatoes*
2 *tablespoons vinegar*
4 *tablespoons vegetable oil*
2 *half chicken breasts*
*chicken stock or water*
2 *cloves garlic, cracked*
1 *bay leaf*
*pinch each rosemary, thyme, sage and parsley*
1 *ripe avocado, peeled and diced*
2 *spring onions finely minced*
2 *tablespoons chopped cress*
1 *tomato, seeded and chopped*

2 *tablespoons lemon juice*          *dash cayenne*
1 *teaspoon dried dill*

1. Dice the unpeeled potatoes and simmer them until just tender. Remove from the cooking liquid.
2. Mix together the vinegar and oil and toss with the still-warm potatoes. Refrigerate for 8–24 hours.
3. Place the chicken breasts in a pot and add the potato cooking water with enough chicken stock or water to cover. Add the garlic, bay leaf, rosemary, thyme, sage and parsley. Cover and simmer until just done.
4. Remove the chicken; skin, bone and dice it and chill.
5. Strain and reserve the cooking liquid.
6. Drain the potatoes. Toss together the potatoes, chicken, avocado, spring onions, cress and tomato.
7. Mix the lemon juice with 2 tablespoons of the reserved cooking liquid (save the rest for soup), dill and cayenne. Toss with the salad and serve on a bed of cos lettuce.
*Serves* 2.

## Levantine Potato Salad (Mid-East)

3 *medium potatoes*                    ⅓ *cup minced parsley*
2 *tablespoons raspberry or cid-*      4 *spring onions, chopped*
 *er vinegar*                          1 *teaspoon each dried mint and*
2 *tbs vegetable oil*                   *dill weed*
2 *tbs lemon juice*                    *ground pepper to taste*
1 *clove garlic, chopped finely*       *paprika*

1. Drop potatoes in boiling water to cover. Cook 20 minutes or until tender. Remove from water. Do not peel. Dice while hot.
2. In a glass or stainless steel bowl, toss hot potatoes with the vinegar, oil, lemon juice and garlic. Let cool. Stir occasionally.
3. When the potatoes are cool, toss in the parsley, spring onions, herbs and pepper. Chill.

4. Garnish with a sprinkle of paprika to serve.
   *Serves 4.*

## Cucumber Yogurt Delight (Mid-East)

I hesitated to call this a salad, when it's sometimes listed as soup. Call it whatever you like, but don't miss it!

1 *large cucumber, peeled and seeded*
1 *cup yogurt cheese (p. 188)*
1 *large spring onion, minced*
1 *teaspoon dried mint (2 teaspoons fresh)*
½ *teaspoon dill weed (1 teaspoon fresh)*
2 *oz. seedless white raisins*
*salt and pepper*
*plain yogurt*

1. Slice cucumbers very thin and place in colander.
2. Mix yogurt cheese with spring onion, mint, dill and raisins. Stir in cucumber. Add salt and pepper to taste.
3. The consistency of the salad should be rather creamy. If it is too thick, stir in plain yogurt as desired.
4. Chill at least 1 hour before serving.
   *Serves 4.*

## Chicory-Nectarine Salad (Americas)

A most colourful and sophisticated combo.

4 *ox. chicory leaves, washed and torn*
1 *cup bean sprouts*
1 *medium tomato in thin wedges*
1 *nectarine, in sections*
1 *tablespoon lemon juice*
*few red onion rings*

DRESSING
¼ *cup vinegar, preferably raspberry*
2 *tablespoons oil, preferably hazelnut*

1. Toss chicory and bean sprouts together with half of the dressing.

2. Arrange the tomato on top. Toss the nectarine sections with lemon juice. Arrange on top of the tomato. Top with the onion rings.
3. Drizzle the remaining dressing over the salad.
*Serves 4.*

## Cabbage and Sprout Salad (Americas)

1 *small head red cabbage, fine-*
*ly shredded*
1 *or 2 cups sprouts — use any*
*favourite, or a mixture*

¼ *pint light vegetable oil*
¼ *cup lemon juice or cider vine-*
*gar*
*dash cayenne (optional)*

Just before serving, toss the cabbage and sprouts together to mix very well. Add the lemon juice or vinegar to the oil together with the cayenne, if desired. Stir vigorously with a fork until the mixture appears slightly thickened. Pour about half of the oil mixture over the salad and toss well. Taste for seasoning. Add more of the oil mixture if needed. Refrigerate any leftover dressing in a covered container for up to a week. Vary the dressing by adding any chopped fresh herbs you fancy.
*Serves 4.*

## Tomato-Cucumber Salad (Mid-East)

2 *medium-size tomatoes*
1 *or 2 cucumbers*
2 *tablespoons olive oil*
2 *tablespoon vegetable oil*
1 *tablespoon cider vinegar*
*juice of* 1 *lemon*

1 *tablespoon coarsely chopped*
*fresh parsley*
1 *teaspoon minced fresh mint*
*white pepper*
*mint sprigs for garnish*

1. Slice tomatoes thin. Peel cucumbers only if they are waxed and slice them very thin. Arrange tomatoes and cucumbers on a plate.
2. Mix together the oils, vinegar and lemon juice. Mix vigorously with a fork. Stir in the parsley and mint.

3. Pour the dressing over the tomatoes and cucumbers. Add fresh ground white pepper to taste.
4. Serve immediately or cover and chill.
5. Garnish with mint sprigs.
   *Serves 4.*

## Cucumber Raita (India/Pakistan)

Raita is served with curries to quench their fire, but it's a delightful salad on its own.

2 *medium cucumbers*
1 *cup plain yogurt (or more to taste)*
1 *teaspoon powdered cumin*
*dash cayenne (optional)*

1. If the cucumbers are waxed, peel them.
2. Dice the cucumber and mix with remaining ingredients. Chill before serving.
   *Serves 4.*
NOTE: This is terrific with the addition of fresh, ripe, chopped tomatoes.

## Russian Bean Salad

Try this with a mixture of beans.

3 *oz. dried red kidney beans*
½ *teaspoon salt*
1 *tablespoon cider vinegar*
1 *small onion, finely chopped*
¼ *cup parsley, finely chopped*
3 *tablespoons minced fresh coriander (if available)*
2 *tablespoons oil*
*minced green part of* 1 *spring onion*
*freshly ground white pepper*

1. Soak the beans in water to cover overnight.
2. Add more water if needed and simmer the beans slowly for about an hour or until the beans are tender.
3. Drain the beans (save the liquid and add it to a soup). Rinse the beans and shake in a colander until quite dry.
4. Mix together the salt, vinegar, onion, parsley, corian-

der and oil. Toss the beans with the mixture. Sprinkle with the spring onion and pepper. Chill.
*Serves 4.*

## Tabbouleh-Bulgur Salad (Mid-East)

Because it's easy and scrumptious, this hearty salad is popular world-wide.

3 oz. bulgur wheat
1 small onion, finely chopped
1 spring onion, finely chopped
½ cup chopped fresh parsley (2 tbs dried)
⅓ cup lemon juice
3 tablespoons mint leaves, minced (3 teaspoons dried)
2 fl. oz. olive oil
3 or 4 tomatoes, cut in wedges

1. Soak the bulgur in cold water to cover 30 minutes. Drain, place the bulgur on a cloth and wring out the excess water.
2. Mix the onion, spring onion, parsley and lemon juice. Toss with the bulgur. Refrigerate at least ½ hour.
3. Meanwhile add the mint to the olive oil. Mix with the bulgur mixture just before serving.
4. To serve, mound the bulgur on a plate and garnish with the tomato wedges. The tomatoes can be chopped fine and added to the bulgur mixture.
*Serves 4.*

## Lentil Salad (Mid-East)

This is a basic recipe to which you may add any of your favourite herbs, spices or raw vegetables. As lentils have a rather bland taste, they go well with many other foods.

1¼ pints water
1 small onion (whole)
1 bay leaf
1 garlic clove
6 oz. lentils
3 tablespoons peanut oil
1 medium, chopped onion
⅓ cup chopped parsley
2 tablespoons cider vinegar
1 tablespoon lemon juice

1. Heat water to boiling. Add small onion, bay leaf and garlic clove. Sprinkle in lentils and simmer covered 25–30 minutes or until lentils are just tender.
2. Drain lentils, rinse with cold water to cool and remove onion, bay leaf, and garlic.
3. Heat the peanut oil in a small frying pan. Sauté minced onion until just transparent. Remove from heat and let cool.
4. Place lentils in large bowl, add sautéed onion, including oil. Mix well. Add parsley, vinegar and lemon juice. Toss to mix well.

*Serves 4.*

# Mustard Facts

World production of mustard seeds is between 350,000 and 280,000 metric tons per year, combining black, brown and white (or yellow) mustard seeds. Black seeds are used in India and Pakistan as an oilseed and, whole, as a condiment in cooking. Whole white seeds are readily available in Britain where their preservative qualities are put to good use in pickling spice mixtures and homemade pickle recipes.

Nearly all of the remaining mustard seed crop is used to make prepared mustard. While even the most pedestrian of food sellers will stock two or three varieties, there are hundreds of styles and flavours to choose from. Some mustards are quite straightforward, while others put ingredients together in an almost whimsical manner. Ranging from bland to sweet to diabolically hot, mustard is surely a condiment with something for everyone's taste.

## Mustard Seeds

**White, yellow, brown:** *Sinapis alba*, sometimes *brassica alba*. Whole white seeds are used for pickling and sprouting. As sprouts, they have a delightful peppery taste.

Available in most supermarkets.

**Black:** *Sinapis negra, brassica negra*. Whole black seeds and an oil derived from them are used in the cooking of India and Pakistan.

Available in ethnic and up-market grocery shops.

## Mustard Powder

Mustard powder is a blend of white and yellow or brown seeds finely ground and mixed with a little flour. Colman's has been producing mustard in this country since 1814.

Available in most supermarkets and grocery shops.

## Prepared Mustards

Ready-to-use mustards can be used either in cooking or as a table condiment. For cooking, smooth mustards, such as Dijon, are preferred.

**Dijon mustard** is strong, but not overly aromatic, so it works well with other flavours and is used extensively in cooking. It is made from a mixture of seeds.

**Moutarde de Meaux** is a coarse mustard in which the seeds are not entirely ground. It is made from a mixture of seeds, and can be used in cooking. It is excellent in salad dressings.

**German mustard** is usually a smooth blend of brown and white seeds, often with a distinctively sweet flavour. Some brands are very hot, others are milder.

**Novelty mustards** can be smooth or coarse, sharp or mild. Some very good ones are made with green peppercorns. Since mustards can be prepared with wine or vinegar, and almost any combination of herbs and spices, the possibilities are nearly limitless.

**Chinese mustard** is made by mixing mustard powder with cold water to make a smooth paste. Let stand 15 minutes before serving. Keeps 2 or 3 hours.

**English mustard** may refer to any of a number of prepared mustards, but can also mean a paste made the same way as Chinese mustard. Milk or beer is sometimes used in place of water.

## Uses for Prepared Mustard

1. Smear on meat, fish, poultry or vegetables before grilling or barbecuing.
2. Add to cheese sauces, white sauces, macaroni and cheese casseroles.
3. Stir into prepared mayonnaise or salad dressing.
4. Stir into cream soups.
5. Blend into dip recipes or thin with yogurt to make a dip for crudités.
6. Mix with wheat germ and bread crumbs for a casserole topping.

## Homemade mustard

Among the pleasures of making mustard is the opportunity to experiment with the seasonings and flavours you enjoy. Texture can be whatever one wishes and salt may be added or omitted.

There is one essential rule to mustard-making: *mustard must be initially mixed with COLD water.* The reason for this is that mustard is not "hot" until the enzymes (glucosides) are activated by cold water. Hot water, vinegar and salt all kill these enzymes. That's why adding dry mustard to your recipe while making mayonnaise will add a bitter note. The vinegar in the recipe kills the "hot" enzymes. The mustard will then be bitter and mild and not very pleasant. However, once the "hot" enzyme has been developed with cold water (15 minutes for powder, 3 hours for whole seeds), almost any flavouring may be added.

A pinch of powdered turmeric is often added to give mustard a yellow colour. Use sparingly, as tumeric can produce both a harsh colour and a bitter taste.

Mustard should be allowed to "rest" 4–5 days after preparation to bring out the best flavour.

Homemade mustard will keep quite well, refrigerated and tightly covered, for at least a year. However, it is best when used within six months.

**NOTE:** In the following recipes a smallish teacup should be used to measure. Measurements need only be approximate.

### Basic Spiced Mustard

⅓ cup white mustard seeds
¼ cup dry mustard
½ cup cold water
1 cup cider vinegar
1 small onion, minced
2 cloves garlic, minced

2 tablespoons honey
½ teaspoon ground cinnamon
¼ teaspoon each ground allspice, mace, ginger
pinch turmeric (optional)

1. Mix mustard seeds, mustard and water. Let stand at least 3 hours.

2. Mix all remaining ingredients in a small enamel or stainless steel saucepan. Bring to a boil. Simmer 5 minutes. Strain. Add liquid to mustard.
3. Place mustard mixture in a blender and blend to desired consistency.
4. Cook mustard mixture in a double boiler over simmering water. Stir and cook for about 10 minutes or until as thick as you like. Mustard will thicken slightly when cool.

   To thin: add a little more vinegar.

   *Makes about 6 ounces.*


## Sweet-Hot Mustard

½ cup white mustard seeds  
2 tablespoons dry mustard  
½ cup cold water  
½ cup white wine  
½ cup white wine vinegar  
½ cup minced onion  

3 cloves garlic, pressed  
1 bay leaf  
8 juniper berries  
⅛ teaspoon ground allspice  
½ teaspoon honey  
honey to taste  

1. Mix mustard seeds, mustard and water. Let stand at least 3 hours.
2. Mix wine, vinegar, onion, garlic, spices and ½ teaspoon honey in small enamel or stainless steel saucepan. Bring to a boil. Simmer over low heat 12 minutes. Strain. Add liquid to mustard mixture.
3. Place mustard mixture in a blender and blend to desired consistency.
4. Cook mustard mixture in a double boiler over simmering water. Stir and cook for about 10 minutes, stirring in 1 to 2 tablespoons honey, or to taste.

   *Makes about 6 ounces.*


## Tarragon Mustard

¼ cup black mustard seeds  
¼ cup white mustard seeds  

¼ cup dry mustard  
¾ cup cold water

¼ cup white wine      2 teaspoons prepared horse-
¼ cup white wine vinegar      radish
1 teaspoon dried tarragon      ⅛ teaspoon allspice

1. Mix mustard seeds, mustard and water. Let stand at least 3 hours.
2. Mix wine, vinegar, tarragon, horseradish and allspice. Heat to boiling. Strain.
3. Add wine mixture to mustard. Blend to desired smoothness.
4. Cook mustard mixture in top of double boiler to desired consistency.
*Makes about 6 ounces.*

## Lemon Mustard

⅓ cup white mustard seeds      juice of 1 large lemon
¼ cup dry mustard      1 tablespoon honey
½ cup water      2 tablespoons white wine
2 tablespoons grated lemon      3 tablespoons white wine vine-
zest      gar

1. Soak mustard seeds, mustard and water for at least 3 hours.
2. Heat lemon zest, lemon juice, honey and white wine to boiling.
3. Add lemon mixture to mustard. Blend to desired smoothness.
4. Cook mixture in top of a double boiler, stirring in vinegar until desired flavour and consistency is achieved.
*Makes about 6 ounces.*

## Basic Mustard Salad Dressing

¼ cup white wine vinegar      1 tablespoon mustard
¾ cup good vegetable oil

The flavour and texture of this very simple dressing depends entirely on the type of mustard used. Dijon is very good, but the coarser mustards are more interesting. Mix all ingredients with a fork until creamy. Refrigerate unused portions.

*To vary: Add herbs, fresh or dried, to taste.*

# Cheese & Egg Main Courses

## Barbara's Manicotti (Italian)

A celebration of cheese.

CRÊPES

| | |
|---|---|
| ¼ lb. whole-wheat flour | 2 eggs, lightly beaten |
| 1 cup water (approx.) | oil or butter |
| ½ teaspoon salt | |

FILLING

| | |
|---|---|
| 1 lb. ricotta cheese | 2 eggs, lightly beaten |
| 14 oz. fresh beancurd (tofu) | ½ teaspoon salt |
| 4 oz. grated mozzarella cheese | 4 tablespoons chopped fresh |
| ¼ cup freshly grated Parmesan | parsley |
| cheese | dash freshly ground white pepper |

SAUCE

| | |
|---|---|
| 3½ cups cooked or tinned tomatoes (with liquid) | 2 cloves garlic, chopped |
| 1 tablespoon oil | 1 teaspoon minced fresh basil (¼ teaspoon dry) |
| 1 cup chopped onion | 1 tablespoon tomato paste |

GARNISH

¼ cup freshly grated Parmesan
   cheese

1. Mix the whole-wheat flour, water, salt and 2 eggs together until smooth. Refrigerate 1 hour.
2. Chop the tomatoes for the sauce. Heat the 1 tablespoon oil in a large pan, and sauté the onion and garlic until limp. Stir in the tomatoes with their liquid, basil and tomato paste. Bring to a boil and cook, stirring often, about 20 minutes or until thick.

3. Beat together the ricotta, bean curd, mozzarella and Parmesan for the filling (or blend in a food processor). Beat or blend in the egg, salt, parsley and pepper. Keep cool until ready to use.

4. Wipe a hot 7″ frying pan with oil over moderate heat. Add a scant quarter-cup of batter to the frying pan and tilt it quickly to cover the bottom with batter. If the batter if too thick, it won't run fast enough. Any "holes" left in the pan can be "patched" with a drop of batter. Cook until the edges appear dry and the batter is "set" in the centre. Lift the crêpe gently with a spatula and set aside.

   Repeat until all the batter is used.

   *Makes about 12 crêpes.*

NOTE *Wiping* the pan with oil ensures a non-stick surface. Excess oil produces a lacy, fragile crêpe that will fall apart.

Swirling the batter in the pan takes only a bit of practice. Right-handed beginners might try pouring batter with the left hand while tilting the pan with the right. Lefties do the opposite.

Crêpes are cooked on one side only.

Unused crêpes may be frozen in a stack, well-wrapped with paper between the layers.

5. Place about ⅓ of the tomato sauce in the bottom of a large baking dish. Preheat oven to 350°F.

6. Holding one crêpe in your left hand (if you are right-handed) place about 3 tablespoons of the filling along one edge, leaving about one inch of crêpe on that side.

7. Roll short edge of crêpe over filling, then wide edge. Place, seam side down, in the prepared baking dish.

8. When all crêpes are filled, top with the remaining sauce and garnish with the extra Parmesan. Bake 45 minutes or until cheese is melted and sauce is bubbly.

   *Serves 4.*

## Greek Macaroni Bake

Easy and very tasty.

½ *lb uncooked whole grain*    ½ *teaspoon pepper*
  *macaroni*                   ½ *teaspoon nutmeg*
1 *tablespoon tahini*         8 *oz. feta cheese*
2 *eggs, lightly beaten*

1. Cook the macaroni in boiling salted water until *al dente*. Drain. Rinse with cold water to cool. Toss with the remaining ingredients.
2. Heat oven to 375°F. Oil a baking dish.
3. Place macaroni mixture in baking dish. Bake 30 minutes or until lightly browned.
   *Serves 4–6.*


## Lasagne (Italian)

Spinach lasagne is recommended for this excellent lasagne.

2–3 *cups Sauce Bolognese (p.*    5 *oz. mozzarella or scamorze*
  *106)*                          *cheese, in small slices*
⅓ *lb. lasagne noodles, cooked* al    1 *lb. fresh ricotta cheese*
  *dente, and drained*         ⅓ *cup freshly grated Parmesan*
                              *cheese*

1. Heat oven to 350°F. Oil an oven-proof baking dish 8–10 inches wide and about 14 inches long.
2. Place a layer of sauce in the bottom of the dish, using about ⅓ of the sauce. Add a layer of lasagne. Make a layer of cheeses, using half of the ricotta, and ⅓ each of the mozzarella and Parmesan. Cover with ⅓ of the sauce.
3. Add a layer of lasagne and repeat the layers of cheese and sauce. Top with the remaining mozzarella and Parmesan and bake for about 45 minutes or until browned and bubbly.
   *Serves 6.*

## Courgette Lasagne (Not Quite Italian)

Lasagne inspired this wonderful vegetable casserole.

1½ *lb. courgettes*
½ *cup whole-wheat bread crumbs*
1 *lb. dry cottage cheese*
2 *tbs. bran (optional)*
½ *teaspoon basil*
¼ *teaspoon oregano*
¼ *teaspoon garlic powder*

2 *tablespoons chopped parsley*
*salt and white pepper to taste*
3–4 *tomatoes, sliced*
¾ *cup shredded mozzarella cheese*
¼ *cup coarsely grated Parmesan cheese*

1. Slice the courgettes ¼″ thick, lengthwise. Place a layer of these strips in the bottom of a dish about 9″ × 9″ × 2″ and sprinkle with half of the breadcrumbs.
2. Mix the cottage cheese together with the bran, basil, oregano, garlic, parsley and salt and pepper. Top the courgette slices with half of this mixture and cover with tomato slices. Add another layer of courgettes, then the remaining crumbs and cottage cheese mixture. Cover with the remaining tomato slices.
3. Mix together the Parmesan and mozzarella and sprinkle over the tomato slices.
4. Bake at 350°F. for 45 minutes, or until the cheese is golden and bubbling. Serve hot.
   *Makes 6 servings.*

## Cheddar Custard (Great Britain)

This is a steamed, savoury custard with a silky texture. Pressure cooking makes it quick to make.

2 *medium eggs*
2 *cup plain yogurt*
½ *teaspoon Dijon mustard*

3 *oz. grated Cheddar cheese*
*salt and pepper to taste*

1. Pour 8 fl. oz. water into pressure cooker. Insert trivet. Begin heating.

2. Butter the inside of a dish that will fit in your cooker, about 3 inches deep.
3. Whisk the eggs until frothy. Stir in the remaining ingredients in the order given. Pour mixture into the prepared dish.
4. Cover the dish with greaseproof paper and fasten tightly.
5. Lower dish into rack. Bring to pressure. Cook 12 mins. *Serves 2.*

## Soufflé Roulade Farcie (French)

FILLING

1 *tablespoon oil or butter*          4 *oz. yogurt cheese or Quark*
½ *medium onion, chopped*          *salt and pepper to taste*
4 *oz. mushrooms, chopped*          *dash freshly grated nutmeg*
1 *cup cooked, chopped spinach*

1. Heat oil or butter and sauté the onions until they're translucent. Add the mushrooms and cook over low heat until the mushrooms are soft.
2. Squeeze the excess moisture from the spinach. Mix the spinach and all remaining ingredients into the onion/mushroom mixture.
3. Allow the filling to cook while you prepare the soufflé.

SOUFFLÉ

2 *oz. butter or oil*          ¾ *pint skimmed milk*
2 *oz. whole wheat flour*          5 *eggs, separated*
½ *teaspoon salt*          2 *tablespoons melted butter for*
⅛ *teaspoon white pepper*          *garnish*

1. Butter a 15½" × 10½" × 1" swiss roll pan. Line the pan with greaseproof paper, butter the paper and dust lightly with flour. Heat oven to 350°F.
2. Melt the butter in a saucepan and whisk in the flour, salt, and pepper. Whisk in the skimmed milk and stir

over moderate heat until thickened. Add a bit of the mixture to the egg yolks. Off the heat, beat the yolks into the milk mixture. Set aside.

3. Beat egg whites until stiff but not dry. Stir about ⅓ of the whites into the yolk mixture. Fold the remaining whites in gently. Using a spatula, smooth into the prepared pan.

4. Bake 15 minutes or until puffy and lightly browned.

5. Remove the pan from the oven and cover with a tea towel larger than the pan. Invert the soufflé onto the towel and let cool for a few minutes. Trim ½″ from short sides.

6. Spread the filling evenly over the soufflé, leaving a 1″ margin. Using the towel, roll the soufflé firmly from the short end.

7. Butter a gratin dish or baking sheet long enough to hold the soufflé. Gently roll the soufflé onto the prepared dish, seam side down, if possible. Brush with the melted butter.

8. Bake the rolled soufflé 12 minutes at 350°F. Place under the grill briefly to brown, if desired. Serve hot or warm.

## Malfatti (Italian)

Malfatti are savoury little dumplings of spinach and cheese to enjoy with tomato sauce.

1 *large bunch fresh spinach (about 8 oz.)*

12 *oz. ricotta cheese*

4 *eggs, beaten*

¼ *cup freshly grated Parmesan cheese*

1 *cup dry, fine whole-wheat bread crumbs*

2 *teaspoons chopped fresh basil (1 teaspoon dried)*

1 *small onion, finely chopped*

2 *cloves garlic, squished through a press*

2 *tablespoons powdered lecithin (optional)*

1 *tablespoon fresh parsley, minced*

1 *teaspoon salt*

¼ *teaspoon pepper*

¼ *teaspoon nutmeg (optional)*

4 *oz. whole-wheat flour*

1. Wash the spinach well. Place it (*not* drained) in a very heavy pan with about 2 tablespoons water. Cover and steam for 5 minutes. The spinach should be just wilted. Mince the spinach finely, and squeeze out as much moisture as possible. (Save the juice for soup).
2. Mix the spinach with the remaining ingredients, omitting the flour. Mix well. Add $\frac{1}{2}$ of the flour. Mix well. Add the remaining flour, a little at a time, until the mixture is fairly stiff. Chill for 2–3 hours.
3. Heat water to boiling in a large pot. Add a little salt. Drop 1–1$\frac{1}{2}$" balls of the spinach-cheese mixture into the boiling water and remove them with a slotted spoon when they rise to the top. Serve hot with tomato sauce.

*Serves 4.*

## Welsh Rarebit (Great Britain)

Served over toasted wholewheat bread, it's a simple, tasty meatless meal.

| | |
|---|---|
| 8 *oz. mature Cheddar, grated* | *pinch each paprika, pepper* |
| 2 *oz. butter* | 8 *fl. oz. stale beer (milk may* |
| 2 *teaspoons prepared mustard* | *be substituted)* |
| *dash Worcestershire sauce* | 2 *tablespoons lecithin powder* |

1. Warm the beer or milk with the butter. Add all the other ingredients and stir until smooth.
2. Pour the cheese mixture over toasted bread and grill until brown and bubbly.

*Four servings.*

## Aubergine Parmigiano (Italian)

One of the world's great vegetarian dishes.

2 *aubergines, unpeeled*
1 *tablespoon olive oil*
1 *onion, minced*
3 *ripe tomatoes, peeled, seeded and chopped*

1 *tablespoon minced fresh basil*
  (*1 teaspoon dry*)
2 *oz. grated Parmesan cheese*
¼ *lb. mozzarella cheese, grated*

1. Slice the aubergines about ½" thick. Place on a rack above boiling water, cover and steam about 20 minutes, or until aubergines are soft.
2. While the aubergines are steaming, heat the olive oil in a frying pan. Briefly sauté the onion. Add the tomatoes and basil. Cook over low heat about 10 minutes to make a thick sauce. Stir occasionally.
3. Heat oven to 350°F.
4. Oil a large, shallow baking dish. Pave the bottom of the dish with a layer of aubergine. Spread with some of the tomato sauce and some of each cheese. Add another layer of aubergine, then tomato sauce and cheese. There should not be more than three layers of aubergine, and two is ideal. The top layer will be cheese.
5. Bake about 40 minutes, or until cheese is bubbly. Serve hot.
   *Serves 4.*

## Enchiladas (Mexico)

Here's a hearty and delicious version of one of Mexico's best vegetarian entrées. As a bonus the dish reheats well and can be frozen.

FILLING

3 *tablespoons oil*
1 *onion, minced*
1 *green pepper, seeded and chopped*

2 *leafy celery stalks, chopped*
3 *cloves garlic, chopped*
1 *tablespoon mild chili powder*
*dash cumin powder*

3 cups cooked beans

2 tablespoons cider vinegar

2 teaspoons salt

SAUCE

4 large, ripe tomatoes, peeled and chopped

1 small onion, chopped

1 clove garlic, chopped

½ teaspoon crushed red pepper, or to taste*

½ teaspoon cumin powder

¼ cup yogurt cheese

1 cup grated Cheddar cheese

8–12 corn tortillas

1. **For the filling:** Heat the oil and sauté the onion, pepper, celery and garlic until soft. Add the chili powder, cumin, cooked beans, vinegar and salt. Mix well, mashing the beans slightly. Heat thoroughly and set aside. Keep warm.
2. **For the sauce:** Heat the tomatoes, onion, garlic, red pepper and cumin powder together in a large frying pan for about 10 minutes or until well blended. One at a time, briefly dip the tortillas in the sauce to soften. Set aside.
3. Stir the yogurt cheese into the sauce. Heat oven to 350°F. Oil a baking dish. Place about 3 tablespoons filling on each tortilla and roll up. Place tortillas in baking dish. When all tortillas are in the dish, top with the sauce. Sprinkle with the grated cheese and bake for about 15 minutes or until sauce is bubbly and cheese has melted. Serve with a green salad.

*Serves 4.*

* Soak in warm water ⅓ hour, drain.

## Omelet Piquante (Americas)

An omelet with a distinctive Latin-American flair.

SOFRITO

1 *tablespoon oil*
1 *small onion, chopped finely*
1 *small tomato, seeded and chopped*
½ *green pepper, chopped*
1 *clove garlic, squished*

2 *teaspoons minced fresh coriander leaves (1 teaspoon dried)*
1 *teaspoon chopped fresh oregano (½ teaspoon dried)*
*dash hot pepper sauce (optional)*

GARNISHES

*sliced mild cheese (Edam, Gouda, mild Cheddar, etc.)*

1 *ripe avocado, peeled and sliced*
8 *eggs*

1. Heat the oil and add the remaining *sofrito* ingredients. Cook over low heat until mushy. Set aside.
2. For each serving make a 2-egg omelet and fill with about 2 tablespoons of the *sofrito* and a few slices of cheese and avocado. Garnish finished omelets with remaining cheese and avocado slices.
   *Makes 4 servings.*

## Baked Eggs California

Serve this exciting dish for breakfast, lunch *or* dinner!

SALSA

1 *small tomato, chopped*
3 *tablespoons chopped onion*
1 *clove garlic, chopped*
2 *fresh or tinned chili peppers (or to taste) seeded and minced\**

2 *tablespoons fresh coriander leaves*
2 *tablespoons vinegar*

\* Chilis are HOT, so use to taste. For a mild version, use ½ green pepper, minced.

GARNISH

juice of ½ lemon ½ cup bean sprouts
½ avocado, sliced few coriander leaves

1 large baking potato, baked 4 eggs
and sliced 2 fl. oz. stock
2–3 thin slices onion

1. Combine all ingredients for *salsa*.
2. Heat oven to 350°F. Butter a shallow baking dish (about 8″ diameter).
3. Arrange potatoes in a layer in baking dish. Top with onion slices. Spoon about half the *salsa* over the onion. Break one egg onto a saucer and slide into the baking dish. Repeat with remaining eggs. Add the stock.
4. Bake the eggs 10–15 minutes or until done. Top with remaining *salsa*.
5. Toss together the garnish ingredients and top the egg dish.
   *Makes 4 portions.*

## Semi-Classic Quiche (Not Quite French)

4 teaspoons Dijon mustard 4 eggs, lightly beaten
prepared crust for one-crust pie 1 cup yogurt
2 teaspoons oil ¼ teaspoon white pepper
1 medium onion, chopped 3 tablespoons bacon-flavoured
1 cup Gruyère cheese, grated bits (optional)
½ cup Cheddar cheese, grated

1. Heat oven to 450°F.
2. Spread mustard over bottom of prepared crust and bake 5 minutes. Remove.
3. Heat the oil and sauté the onion until soft. Spread into the crust. Top with the Gruyère and Cheddar cheeses.
4. Mix the eggs with the yogurt and pepper. Pour over the cheeses.
5. Bake 15 minutes. Reduce heat to 350°F. and bake 10

minutes more or until knife inserted 1″ from the edge comes out clean.

6. Sprinkle with bacon-flavoured bits, if desired.


## Pizza Quiche (Not Quite Italian)

An interesting and delectable variation on the ever-popular quiche.

½ *tablespoon oil*
1 *small onion, chopped*
2 *cloves garlic, chopped*
3 *medium tomatoes, peeled, seeded and chopped*
2 *teaspoons tomato paste*
1 *teaspoon dried basil*
½ *teaspoon dried oregano*
*dash cayenne*

*pinch powdered fennel seed*
*prepared crust for one-crust pie*
1 *teaspoon oil*
10 *small mushrooms, sliced*
½ *cup grated Cheddar cheese*
1 *cup yogurt*
3 *eggs, lightly beaten*
4 *oz. mozzarella cheese, sliced thin*

1. Heat the ½ tablespoon oil and sauté the onion, garlic and tomatoes until soft and thick. Stir in the tomato paste, basil, oregano, cayenne and fennel. Set aside.
2. Heat oven to 450°F. Bake crust 5 minutes. Remove.
3. Heat 1 teaspoon oil and sauté the mushrooms until soft.
4. Spread the onion/tomato mixture into the prepared crust. Add the mushrooms and grated Cheddar.
5. Beat together the yogurt and eggs and pour over the pie. Top with the sliced mozzarella.
6. Bake 15 minutes. Lower heat to 350°F. and bake 10 minutes more or until knife inserted 1″ from edge comes out clean.

# Fish

## Red Snapper Veracruz

Here's a delicious variation on a Mexican favourite. Any firm-fleshed white fish may be substituted.

SALSA (SAUCE)

2 tablespoons oil
1 large onion, chopped
4 tomatoes, peeled, seeded and chopped
2 cloves garlic, chopped finely
2 tablespoons lime or lemon juice
$\frac{1}{4}$ cup sliced green olives
$\frac{1}{8}$ teaspoon cinnamon
pinch allspice
$1\frac{1}{2}$ lbs. red snapper (or other fish) fillets
3 tablespoons wheat germ oil

1. Heat the 2 tablespoons oil. Add the onion and cook over moderate heat until onion is soft. Add remaining ingredients for the *Salsa*. Cook over low heat, stirring occasionally, until mixture is fairly thick.
   NOTE: This part may be done in advance.
2. Rinse the fillets and pat dry. Dip them in wheat germ to coat.
3. Heat grill. Oil a shallow baking dish. Arrange the fillets in the dish in one layer. Grill, turning once, until fish is opaque (about 3 minutes each side, depending on thickness).
4. Remove the cooked fillets to a warm platter and top with the warm sauce.
   *Serves 4.*

## Fillet of Sole Veronique (French)

A marvellous marriage of sea and vineyard.

2 *tablespoons chopped spring
  onions*
4 *large or 8 small sole fillets
  (about 1½ lbs.)*
*salt and pepper to taste*
½ *pint dry white wine*

1 *tablespoon lemon juice*
12 *oz. green seedless grapes*
1 *oz. butter (optional)*
2 *teaspoons cornflour mixed
  with 3 teaspoons water*

NOTE: This dish is traditionally made with an abundance of butter and cream, which we have omitted. If you prefer a richer dish, add ¼ cup double cream and 1 more ounce butter to the finished sauce.

1. Cut a piece of greaseproof paper to make a circle slightly smaller than the lid of an enamelled or stainless steel frying pan. Cut a small hole in the centre of the round.
2. Sprinkle the spring onions onto the frying pan. Fold the fillets in half to form wedge shapes and arrange in the frying pan with the fold toward the outside. Sprinkle with salt and pepper. Add the wine and lemon juice. Add the water to *just* cover the fillets. Top with the prepared greaseproof paper.
3. Bring to a boil. Simmer about 5 minutes or until fish flakes easily. Carefully remove fish to a warm serving platter.
4. Add the grapes to the liquid in the frying pan. Cook to heat through — 2 to 3 minutes — and remove with a slotted spoon. Arrange grapes on fillets.
5. Boil liquid remaining in the frying pan over high heat until reduced to about 1 cup. Whisk in the butter and the cornflour paste. Spoon this sauce over the fillets. *Serves 4.*

## Fish with Tahini Sauce (N. African)

Simple to prepare and wonderful to taste.

1 *tablespoon vegetable oil*
1 *large onion, chopped*
1 *lb. fish fillets*
*salt (optional)*

1–2 *cloves garlic*
2 *tablespoons tahini sauce*
  *(sesame seed paste)*
2 *tbs. lemon juice*

1. Heat the vegetable oil in a large frying pan. Sauté the onion over moderate heat until soft but not browned. Set aside.
2. Heat oven to 350°F.
3. Spread the onions in a baking dish large enough to hold the fillets in one layer. Add the fillets. Sprinkle with a little salt, if desired.
4. Bake the fish and onions 10 minutes.
5. While the fish is baking, crush the garlic (a mortar works well for this), stir in the tahini and lemon juice and mix to blend well.
6. Spread the fish with the tahini mixture and bake 10–20 minutes more (depending on thickness of fillets) or until fish flakes easily with a fork.
*Serves 6.*

## Truite au Bleu

One of the greatest of French dishes.

4 *trout (trout should be cleaned*
  *as it is caught, but the*
  *head should not be removed)*
1½ *pints water*
¾ *pint white wine*
1 *leafy sprig celery*

1 *carrot*
1 *onion*
6 *peppercorns*
1 *small bay leaf*
1 *teaspoon salt*

Heat the water to a boil in a large pan. Add the wine, celery, carrot, onion, peppercorns, bay leaf and salt. (You have just made a *court-bouillon*). When the *court-bouillon* resumes boiling, add the trout and let them poach for 4–5 minutes. Remove from the *court-bouillon*.

Serve on a warm platter with small boiled potatoes and melted butter.

*Serves 4.*

## Fish Souvlakia (Mid-East)

Fish kebabs are excellent. If you're planning a barbecue or picnic, transport the fish in the marinade and drain just before threading on skewers.

MARINADE

| | |
|---|---|
| 2 *tablespoons oil (olive oil is good)* | 2 *spring onions, minced* |
| $\frac{1}{3}$ *cup dry vermouth or white wine* | $1\frac{1}{2}$ *lbs. firm-fleshed fish steaks in cubes about 2″ × 2″ × $\frac{3}{4}$″* |
| 2 *tbs. fresh lemon juice* | *cherry tomatoes* |
| $\frac{1}{2}$ *teaspoon salt* | *mushroom caps* |
| 1 *teaspoon dried oregano* | *spring onions in 2″ pieces* |
| 2 *cloves garlic, crushed* | *lemon wedges* |
| | *parsley* |

1. Marinate the fish overnight, refrigerated.
2. Drain, reserve marinade. Thread on skewers alternating with cherry tomatoes, mushroom caps, spring onion (or any pleasing combination).
3. Grill 10 minutes, turning occasionally and basting with the reserved marinade.
4. Serve garnished with lemon wedges and parsley.
   *Serves 4.*

## Tuna Sauce for Pasta (Italian) (Tonnato)

A quick and delectable sauce for your favourite pasta.

| | |
|---|---|
| $\frac{1}{2}$ *medium onion, chopped fine* | $\frac{1}{4}$ *pint chicken stock or water* |
| 1 *clove garlic, chopped fine* | 1 *large tin tuna ($12\frac{1}{2}$ oz.) drained* |
| 1 *stalk celery, chopped fine* | |

2 *tablespoons lemon juice*  
3 *tablespoons chopped parsley*  
¾–1 *cup yogurt*

4 *teaspoons capers, rinsed and*  
*drained (optional)*  
*hot, cooked pasta*  
*paprika*

1. Heat together the onion, garlic, celery and stock. Cook at a simmer until vegetables are soft. Flake the tuna and add it to the vegetables.
2. In a blender or food processor, purée the tuna mixture to a smooth paste.
3. Heat the tuna paste to boiling. Stir in the lemon juice, 2 tablespoons parsley, ¾ cup yogurt and capers.
4. Toss the pasta with half of the tuna sauce. If desired, thin remaining sauce with remaining yogurt. Pour over the pasta. Garnish with the remaining parsley and paprika.

*Serves 4.*

## Kulebiaka (Russian)

This is really just a very elaborate fish pie, but it's too good to ignore.

1 *recipe sour cream pastry (p. 170)*  
2 *cups cooked, picked-over salmon (or 1 lb. tin, drained)*  
1 *tablespoon oil*  
2 *medium onions, chopped*  
½ *lb. mushrooms, chopped*  
1 *tablespoon dried dill*  
*juice of one small lemon*

1 *cup cooked brown rice*  
2 *hard-boiled eggs, chopped*  
½ *teaspoon freshly ground white pepper*  
1 *teaspoon salt*  
1 *egg yolk with 1 tablespoon cream*  
1 *ounce butter*

1. Drain the salmon thoroughly by letting it stand in a colander about 10 minutes.
2. Heat the oil. Sauté the onions until translucent. Add the mushrooms and sauté briefly. Add the dill and 1 tablespoon of the lemon juice. Remove from heat.
3. Toss the rice with the remaining lemon juice.

4. Roll the pastry on a floured board to make a rectangle about 10″ × 15″. Trim the edges neatly and save the trimmings.

5. In the centre of the dough, make a rectangle of chopped eggs, roughly 4″ × 10″. Cover the eggs with the mushroom-onion mixture and top that with the salmon. Try to make a tall, neat rectangle. Sprinkle the salmon with the salt and pepper. Top the salmon with the rice. Lift the short ends of the dough to cover the ends of the salmon-rice mixture. Wrap the remaining dough to make a neat covering. Place the entire package on a greased baking sheet, seam side down.

6. Roll out the remaining dough scraps and cut them into decorative strips or shapes. Glaze the kulebiaka with some of the yolk-cream mixture and decorate with the dough shapes or strips. Glaze the decorations. Cut a 1″ hole in the top of the kulebiaka. Refrigerate for at least 20 minutes, up to 12 hours.

7. Preheat oven to 375°F. Melt the 1 ounce butter and pour it into the hole in the top of the kulebiaka. Bake the kulebiaka for 15 minutes, lower the heat to 350°F. and bake for about 45 minutes more. The interior should be hot but do not let the crust scorch.

8. To serve: Slice the kulebiaka, cut the slices in half. Serve with melted butter, if desired.
*Serves 6.*

## Scampi (Italian)

Remarkably easy. Serve with hot, cooked rice.

| | |
|---|---|
| 1½ *lbs. large prawns* | 1 *tablespoon* each *butter, olive* |
| *shells from prawns* | *oil, vegetable oil* |
| ¼ *pint white wine* | 2 *cloves garlic, minced* |
| 2 *fl. oz. water* | 1 *tablespoon chopped fresh* |
| 2 *tablespoons lemon juice* | *parsley* |
| *dash pepper* | *salt to taste* |

1. Shell and devein the prawns, setting the shells aside. If possible, leave the shell on the tip of the tail to add colour to the dish. Set the prawns aside.
2. Place the reserved shells in a saucepan with the wine, water, lemon juice and pepper. Simmer 8 minutes, strain. Set liquid aside.
3. Heat the butter and oils in a large frying pan. When foamy, add the prawns and garlic. Stir until the prawns are beginning to turn pink. Add the reserved liquid, parsley and salt to taste. Cook over moderate heat until prawns are cooked through. (The time will depend on the size of the prawns, but should not be more than 4 or 5 minutes). Prawns are done when the flesh is opaque throughout.
4. Remove the prawns with a slotted spoon. Boil the sauce in the pan to reduce to about ½ cup. Spoon over the prawns.

*Serves 4.*

Good with rice.

NOTE: For an extra-low-fat version omit the butter and oil, reduce the garlic to one clove, and cook the prawns in the liquid as above without sautéeing them.


## Coquilles St. Jacques
A French Classic

| | |
|---|---|
| 1 *lb. scallops (about)* | 1½ *oz. butter* |
| 3 *shallots or spring onions, chopped* | ¼ *cup water* |
| | 2 *tablespoons lemon juice* |
| *few sprigs parsley* | 1 *tablespoon oil* |
| 1 *bay leaf* | 1½ *oz. whole wheat flour* |
| *pinch thyme* | *reserved liquid* |
| ½ *cup white wine or stock* | ¼ *cup milk (or more)* |
| *dash salt* | ½ *cup grated Emmenthal or* |
| 10–12 *mushrooms, chopped* | *Gruyere cheese* |

Place the scallops, shallots, parsley, bay leaf, thyme, wine and salt in a pot. Bring to a boil, cover, simmer 5 minutes. Let cool.

Sauté the mushrooms lightly in 1 oz. butter, add the water and lemon juice, cover, simmer 5 minutes. Drain. Reserve the liquid.

Drain the scallops, reserving the liquid. Discard the herbs. Cut the scallops into small pieces if they are large. Mix the scallops with the mushrooms.

Butter or oil 6 large scallop shells or individual ramekins.

Melt $2\frac{1}{2}$ oz. butter with the oil, stir in the flour. Add the reserved liquid from both scallops and mushrooms. Cook to thicken. Add milk to obtain desired thickness. Add the mushrooms and scallops to the sauce. Heat through.* Divide the mixture among the buttered shells. Sprinkle with the cheese and grill until the cheese is melted and slightly brown. Serve hot.

*Serves 6 as an appetizer — 3 as a main dish.*
* May be done ahead to this point.

# Chicken
# and
# Other Poultry

Chicken is one of the favourite foods of people the world over. Although it was once considered a luxury food to be served for festive occasions, chicken has now become an economical source of lean, high-quality protein. Most of the fat in chicken is easily removed and for extra leanness, simply remove the skin before cooking.

Aside from those considerations, however, chicken is one of the most versatile meats available. The flavour of fresh chicken is both subtle enough to mingle well with a variety of seasonings and hearty enough to hold its own in literally thousands of different recipes. (Frozen chicken is distinguished only by its total lack of taste.) Because chickens are raised in relatively little space, require fairly small amounts of feed and grow to edible size in less than two months, chickens have been raised in nearly every part of the world. The result is an international collection of delightful recipes.

Chicken can be boiled, grilled, baked, fried, fricasséed, sautéed, sauced, smothered, skewered, spiced, marinated, moulded, stuffed or stewed. There's virtually no limit to what can be done with chicken. Chicken also poses no leftover problems, because it's an old favourite served cold in salads and sandwiches. Leftover chicken can also be minced and added to soups.

Chicken breasts are available either in pairs or split, with bone in or boneless. For clarity, we call one *half* of a pair of chicken breasts "one breast." In other words, if you were to buy a whole chicken, cut it up, and split the breastbone down the centre, you'd have two breasts. Unless boneless chicken is specified, you may leave the bones in place — we think it adds to the flavour. However, if you'd rather use boneless chicken, remember that it will cook somewhat faster.

## Chicken Cappriccio (Italy)

1 *roasting chicken (3½–4 lbs.)*      2 *cups tomatoes, chopped*
    *cut up*      1 *teaspoon basil*
*vegetable oil (optional)*      ½ *teaspoon oregano*
1 *large onion, chopped*      *pinch fennel*
2 *cloves garlic, crushed*      2 *tablespoons lemon juice*

Optional: Brown the chicken pieces in oil a few at a time until golden.

Combine chicken, onion, garlic, tomatoes, basil, oregano, fennel and lemon juice. Cover and cook at simmer 45 minutes or until done. May be cooked in a slow cooker at LOW for 6 hours.

Serve with cooked pasta
*Serves 4.*

## Chicken Caribe (The Americas)
Succulent and subtly spiced

1 *roasting thicken (3½–4 lbs.)*      1 *clove garlic, minced*
    *cut up*      1 *teaspoon salt*
2 *tablespoons vegetable oil*      ½ *teaspoon cumin powder*
1 *large onion, chopped*      ¼ *teaspoon pepper*
2 *to 3 tomatoes, peeled, seeded*      2 *cup stock*
    *and chopped*      1 *oz. whole wheat flour*
1 *pepper, seeded and diced*

Heat the oil in a frying pan and brown the chicken, a few pieces at a time. Place the browned chicken in the slow cooker. Add the onion, tomatoes, pepper, garlic, salt, cumin, pepper and stock. Cover and cook at simmer 45 minutes. May be cooked in a slow cooker at LOW for 6 hours.

Remove the chicken to a warm platter. Mix $\frac{1}{3}$ cup of the cooking liquid with the whole wheat flour. Stir the flour mixture into the simmering sauce to thicken. Pour over the chicken.

Serve with saffron rice.

*Serves 4.*


## Mexican Marinated Chicken

| | |
|---|---|
| 4 *chicken breasts* | $\frac{1}{2}$ *teaspoon finely minced garlic* |
| 8 *fl. oz. vegetable oil* | 2 *tablespoons wine vinegar* |
| 2 *cloves garlic, crushed* | *dash cayenne pepper (optional)* |
| 1 *bay leaf, crumbled* | 2 *oz. whole wheat flour* |
| 1 *teaspoon oregano* | 1 *medium onion in four thick* |
| $\frac{1}{2}$ *teaspoon paprika* | *slices* |
| 1 *teaspoon lemon juice* | |

Mix together 3 tablespoons oil, the crushed garlic, bay leaf, oregano, paprika and lemon juice. Turn the chicken breasts in the mixture to coat and marinate in a glass bowl, refrigerated, for at least 8 hours, turning chicken occasionally. Combine the minced garlic with the vinegar, 3 tablespoons oil and the cayenne pepper, beat with a fork. Set aside.

Dredge the chicken pieces in the flour.

Heat the remaining oil in a large frying pan and add the chicken breasts, skin side down. Cook until golden, turn and cook until golden on the other side. Add the onion slices and brown them lightly on both sides. Cover the pan and cook over low heat for about 5 minutes more, or until chicken is done. Pour off the oil. Beat the oil and vinegar mixture again then pour it over the chicken. Cover the pan and let stand off heat for 2–3 minutes. Serve hot.

*Serves 4.*

## Chicken Sauté a la Bordelaise (French)

3 *lb. frying chicken, cut up*
6 *tablespoons vegetable oil*
20 *whole, peeled shallots*
1 *tablespoon lemon juice*
1 *bay leaf*

1    9-*oz    package    frozen
    artichoke hearts, defrosted
    and drained*
½ *cup chicken stock*

Sauté the chicken in 4 tablespoons of the vegetable oil until lightly browned. Remove to a platter. Add the shallots to the pan and stir to brown lightly. Pour off the excess oil and return the chicken to the pan. Add the lemon juice and bay leaf, cover the pan and cook at simmer for 30 minutes, or until chicken is tender, basting occasionally.

Heat remaining 2 tablespoons vegetable oil in a heavy pan. Add the artichoke hearts, stir briefly to coat with oil. Cover the pan and cook at simmer for 10 minutes. If the pan seems too dry, add a little lemon juice.

Arrange the cooked chicken and the artichoke hearts on a platter. Remove the bay leaf from the chicken pan and stir in the chicken stock, scraping up all the browned bits from the pan. Bring to a boil and pour (shallots and all) over the chicken and artichoke hearts.

*Serves 4–6.*

## Liz's Chicken

4–6 *chicken breasts*
2 *tablespoons vegetable oil*
1 *large onion, sliced*
2 *cloves garlic, crushed*
8 *oz. mushrooms, sliced*
1 *carrot, grated*

*juice of* ½ *lemon*
2 *cups tomato sauce*
3 *tablespoons red wine or stock*
½ *teaspoon basil*
1 *tablespoon tomato paste*

Sauté the chicken breasts in the oil until lightly browned. Remove to a platter. Add the onion, garlic, mushrooms and carrot to the oil and sauté until the vegetables are limp. Add the lemon juice, cover the pan and let simmer for about 5 minutes. Add the tomato sauce, wine and basil and mix. Add the chicken breasts, cover and simmer for 20 minutes or until the chicken is tender. Remove the chicken to a warm platter. Add the tomato paste to the sauce mixture and cook, stirring, over high heat until the sauce is thickened.

*Serves 4–6.*

## Duck with Calico Stuffing

| | |
|---|---|
| 1 *duck, about 5 lbs., halved* | $\frac{1}{4}$ *teaspoon thyme* |
| *duck giblets* | $\frac{1}{4}$ *cup sunflower seeds* |
| 2 *tablespoons oil* | 1$\frac{1}{2}$ *cups wholewheat bread* |
| 1 *large spanish onion (about $\frac{3}{4}$* | *cubes (about 4 slices)* |
| *lb.) chopped* | $\frac{1}{2}$ *cup duck stock (see below)* |
| 1 *leafy stalk celery, chopped* | *salt and pepper to taste* |
| $\frac{1}{2}$ *lb. dried apricots, chopped* | 2 *tablespoons soy sauce* |

Drop the duck in boiling water to cover for about 10 minutes. Remove and drain. Set aside.

Place the duck giblets in about 2 cups of water. Simmer for about 15 minutes to make stock. Strain the broth.

Heat oven to 325°F. Oil a large baking dish.

Heat the 2 tablespoons oil in a large frying pan. Sauté the onion and celery until translucent. Stir in the apricots, thyme, sunflower seeds, bread cubes, stock, salt and pepper.

Place the duck halves, skin side up, in the oiled baking pan. Bake 10 minutes. Baste with the soy sauce and bake 10 minutes more. Place the stuffing mixture under the duck halves and bake 30 minutes more, or until the duck is done.

*Serves 4.*

## Poulet au Vin Blanc (French)

This chicken in white wine is quick and easy with a light, delicious sauce.

| | |
|---|---|
| 1 *chicken, cut into serving pieces* | ¼ *pint chicken stock* |
| 2 *tablespoons oil* | 2 *tbs. lemon juice* |
| 4 *oz. fresh mushrooms, sliced* | *pinch cayenne* |
| 3 *spring onions, minced* | *pinch thyme* |
| 1 *oz. whole-wheat flour* | 1 *tablespoon arrowroot or cornflour mixed with 2 tablespoons water* |
| ½ *pint dry white wine* | |

1. Fry chicken in oil, 5–6 minutes each side until brown.
2. Add mushrooms and spring onions. Stir.
3. Sprinkle flour evenly over all.
4. Add wine, half the stock, lemon juice, cayenne and thyme. Bring to a boil. Cover and simmer 20 minutes, or until chicken is done.
5. Remove the chicken and mushrooms to a warm platter. Stir the arrowroot mixture into the sauce, stirring until thick. Pour some over the chicken and serve the rest in a separate sauceboat.
*Serves 4.*


## Chicken Hongroise (Hungary)

Paprika-spicy, this Hungarian Chicken sheds its high calorie count when thickened yogurt is substituted for the traditional sour cream.

| | |
|---|---|
| 1 *chicken 3–4 lbs., cut up* | 2 *small containers natural yogurt* |
| 2 *tablespoons vegetable oil* | |
| 2 *medium onions, minced* | 4 *tablespoons chicken stock* |
| 1 *tablespoon medium paprika* | 2 *oz. whole-wheat flour* |
| *juice of 1 lemon* | |

1. Disjoint the chicken and cut into serving pieces. Reserve wingtips, neck, backbone and giblets for stock.
2. Heat the oil and sauté chicken pieces until golden. Add onions, paprika and lemon juice. Toss to mix well. Add 4 tablespoons yogurt and 4 tablespoons stock. Cover tightly and simmer 25 minutes or until chicken is tender.
3. Remove chicken to a warm plate.
4. Whisk the flour into the sauce remaining in the pan. Stir until thick, then stir in the remaining yogurt. Pour over the chicken.

## Chicken Molé

A traditional Mexican dish, molé is so rich, delicious and unusual that I break my "no-chocolate" rule. **Turkey molé** can be made the same way, just extend the time in step 4, cooking the turkey until just barely tender. Two chickens can be used without further changes in the recipe.

MOLÉ SAUCE

2 tablespoons sesame seeds
2 oz. almonds
2 oz. peanuts
2 oz. raisins
2 tablespoons chili powder
$\frac{1}{4}$ teaspoon anise seeds
$\frac{1}{4}$ teaspoon cinnamon
4 cloves
$\frac{1}{4}$ teaspoon coriander

2 large peeled, chopped tomatoes
$\frac{1}{4}$ teaspoon peppercorns
1 oz. grated, bitter chocolate
2 onions, minced
2 cloves garlic, peeled and chopped
2 tablespoons oil
salt to taste

1. Place the sesame seeds, almonds and peanuts in a large

frying pan and toast over moderate heat until the seeds jump. Take care to avoid scorching.

2. Place the toasted mixture in a blender or food processor, add the raisins, chili powder, anise seeds, cinnamon, cloves, coriander, tomatoes, peppercorns and chocolate. Blend as smooth as possible.

3. Mix the onions, garlic and oil. Place in a small, heavy, covered pot and cook over low heat until the onions are limp. Add the onion mixture to the mixture in the blender and blend until smooth. Add salt to taste. Set aside until the chicken has been prepared.

CHICKEN MOLÉ

| | |
|---|---|
| 1 *frying chicken, cut up* | 1 *stalk celery with leaves* |
| 2½ *pints water* | 1 *clove garlic, peeled* |
| 1 *onion, peeled* | *generous pinch oregano* |
| 1 *carrot, scrubbed* | 8 *peppercorns* |
| 1 *bay leaf* | *salt to taste* |

4. Put all ingredients in a large pot. Bring to a boil. Cover and simmer over low heat for 15 minutes.

5. Drain the chicken. Strain and reserve the stock. Return the chicken to the pot.

6. Mix the prepared Molé sauce with ¾ pint of the chicken stock, pour over the chicken. Simmer the mixture for 7 minutes, or until the chicken is done. Do not let it boil. Garnish with more sesame seeds if desired.

7. Chicken Molé may be prepared in advance and reheated in a low (225°F.) oven until warmed through. *Serves 4.*


## Pollo D'Oro (Americas)

Annatto seeds, which often provide the colour for deep yellow cheeses, make this Pollo d'Oro (Chicken of Gold) an attractive dish with a Caribbean flavour.

| | |
|---|---|
| 2 *teaspoons annatto seeds, softened (see glossary)* | 3–4 *cloves garlic, peeled* |
| | ½ *teaspoon dried oregano* |

½ teaspoon cumin seed
½ teaspoon mild or hot paprika
¼ teaspoon cinnamon powder
3 whole cloves
¾ cup fresh orange juice (2
  medium oranges)

¼ cup fresh lemon juice (1
  medium lemon)
juice of one lime
1 chicken cut in serving pieces

1. In a blender or mortar, grind together the annatto seeds, garlic, oregano, cumin, paprika, cinnamon and cloves. Add the juices. Mix well.
2. Rinse the chicken pieces, pat dry, place in a deep bowl and cover with the juice mixture. Cover the bowl and let the chicken marinate in the refrigerator up to 24 hours, turning occasionally.
3. Drain marinade and heat to boiling in large pot. Add chicken pieces, cover and simmer over low heat 1½ hours or until chicken is tender.
4. Serve chicken with hot, cooked brown rice with the sauce on the side.
   *Serves 4.*

## Arroz con Pollo (Americas)

Chicken and rice cooked together appear in many guises around the Caribbean. This dish can be varied by adding about ½ cup of diced ham or smoked sausage in Step 3.

1 chicken, cut up
1 teaspoon salt
½ teaspoon pepper
¼ teaspoon medium paprika
2 tablespoons vegetable oil
1 clove garlic, minced
1 medium onion, chopped
¾ pint chicken broth

2 cups tinned whole tomatoes,
  not drained
1 bay leaf
½ teaspoon dried oregano
¼ teaspoon saffron (optional)
6 oz. raw brown rice
1 cup fresh or frozen peas
1 small jar pimientos, drained
  and diced

1. Rinse the chicken pieces, pat dry. Sprinkle with the salt, pepper and paprika.

2. Heat the oil in pressure cooker or frying pan. Brown the chicken pieces, a few at a time. Set the chicken aside.

3. Stir garlic and onion in the oil remaining in the pan until well coated. Add broth, tomatoes, bay leaf, oregano, saffron and rice. Bring to a boil.

4. OVEN METHOD: Place rice mixture and chicken in ovenproof pot. Cover tightly and bake at 350°F. for 30 minutes. Add peas and pimientos and bake, covered, 10 minutes more.

5. PRESSURE COOKER: Bring rice mixture to pressure, cook 5 minutes, cool quickly.* Add chicken to pot, cover, bring to pressure, cook 10 minutes, cool quickly. Over heat, stir in peas and pimientos and simmer, uncovered, 5 minutes.
*Serves 6.*

* Dish can be prepared in advance to this point. Also reheats well.


## Spanish Chicken Casserole

Here's a hearty, one-dish meal. Most of the cooking can be done in advance. Serve with a green salad and some crusty bread.

CASSEROLE

1 *roasting chicken, 4–5 lbs.*
1 *onion, sliced*
2 *carrots, sliced*
2 *stalks celery, sliced*
2 *tomatoes, peeled, seeded and chopped*

3 *cloves garlic, minced*
1 *teaspoon coarse salt*
½ *teaspoon pepper*
*pinch thyme*

VEGETABLE GARNISH

1 *small head cabbage, cut in 8 sections*

2 *cups cooked chickpeas (garbanzos)*

THICKENING

2 *tablespoons cornflour or arrowroot mixed with 2 tablespoons water*

1. Remove giblets from chicken and use for stock. Place the whole chicken in a large pot with the onion, carrots, celery, tomatoes, garlic, salt, pepper and thyme. Add 1½ pints water. Bring to a boil, cover and simmer over low heat for 45 minutes, or until tender, turning the bird once.*
2. Remove the chicken from the pot and set aside. Purée the cooked vegetables from the stock.
3. Return the purée to the pot. Add the cabbage and chickpeas. Simmer 12 minutes or until the cabbage is just barely tender.
4. If needed, stir the thickening into the simmering purée.
5. Carve the chicken into serving pieces. Place on large platter or deep bowl and top with the vegetables and purée.
*Serves 4.*

* NOTE: Dish may be done 2–3 days ahead at this point.

## Chicken a la Jerez (Spanish)

Jerez is the region of Spain which produces sherry wine and this marvellous recipe thickened with crushed almonds.

| | |
|---|---|
| 2 oz. toasted almonds | 8 fl. oz. chicken stock |
| 2 fl. oz. dry sherry | 2 tablespoons lemon juice |
| 6 cloves garlic | 1 teaspoon lemon zest |
| 2 tablespoons olive oil | 1 chicken, cut in serving pieces |

1. Crush almonds with 1 tablespoon sherry in a mortar or food processor to a rough mixture.
2. Mince the garlic. Heat the olive oil and sauté the garlic until barely golden. Drain, reserving both garlic and oil.
3. Mash the garlic with the almonds. Add 2 tablespoons sherry and the stock, lemon juice and zest.
4. Heat the garlic oil and sauté the chicken pieces until golden. Drain all oil. Add the almond mixture.

5. Cover and simmer 45 minutes or until done *or* PRESS-URE COOK 12 minutes, let cool 5 minutes, run pot under cold water to cool.
*Serves 4.*

## Chicken with Pineapple (Americas)

This Caribbean dish combines lime, pineapple, rum and spices in a rich, intriguing sauce. Wonderful with rice.

1 *chicken, cut in serving pieces*
2 *tbs. lime juice (or lemon)*
3 *tablespoons annatto oil (see glossary) or vegetable oil*
1 *medium onion, chopped*
2 *cloves garlic, chopped*
2 *fl. oz. white wine*
4 *medium tomatoes, peeled, seeded and chopped*

⅓ *cup seedless raisins (white preferred)*
1 *teaspoon grated lime zest (or lemon)*
1 *teaspoon dried oregano*
½ *teaspoon cumin powder*
2 *fl. oz. dark rum, optional*
1 *cup fresh pineapple, finely chopped*

1. Marinate chicken in lime juice 10 minutes. Drain. Reserve juice.
2. Heat annatto oil. Brown chicken pieces a few at a time. Remove to a warm plate. Stir onion and garlic in remaining oil until just soft. Return chicken pieces, any juices accumulated on plate and remaining marinade. Add white wine. Cover and simmer 25 minutes over low heat.
3. Add tomatoes, raisins, lime zest, oregano and cumin to chicken. Cover and simmer 10 minutes more or until chicken is done. Set aside and keep warm.
4. Heat rum. Off heat, touch with a lighted match to flame. When flame subsides, stir in pineapple. (This step may be omitted).
5. Remove chicken to a warm serving platter. Heat the sauce remaining in the pot to boiling. Stir in the pineapple. Pour over the chicken. Serve hot.
*Serves 4.*

## Chicken with Peaches (Mid-East)

When the first peaches arrive in the market, they aren't always thoroughly ripe. Here's a delectable way to use those early, tart peaches. Very good with steamed rice and a salad.

1 *chicken*
2 *tablespoons clarified butter, or oil*
1 *medium onion, chopped coarsely*
1 *teaspoon turmeric*
½ *pint chicken stock*
1 *cinnamon stick*
*juice of* 1 *lemon*
2 *cups sliced peaches (see Note)*

1. Cut the chicken into serving pieces. Use bakc, neck and wingtips for stock. Rinse chicken pieces with cold water and pat dry with paper towels.
2. Heat the butter or oil in a heavy pan. Brown the chicken, a few pieces at a time. Remove chicken.
3. Stir onion and turmeric in the oil remaining in the pan. Stir over moderate heat until onion is limp.
4. Stir in the stock, scraping up all the browned bits. Return the chicken to the pot. Add the cinnamon stick. Cover and simmer over low heat 35 minutes.
5. Stir the lemon juice into the chicken mixture. Add the peaches, but do not stir. Cover and simmer 25 minutes. *Serves 4.*

NOTE: Use either fresh, *almost* ripe peaches, peeled and stoned, sliced and tossed with lemon juice OR tinned peaches in natural juice, drained and rinsed.

## Pakistani Style Barbecued Chicken

A simple, flavourful marinade transforms ordinary chicken into a tender, flavourful delight. The yogurt in the marinade tenderises the meat while retaining all its juiciness.

1 *chicken, about* 4 *lbs.*

MARINADE

1 *cup yogurt*
1 *slice fresh ginger (¼ teaspoon powdered)*
2 *or* 3 *cloves of garlic*

½ *teaspoon cayenne*
1 *teaspoon lemon juice*
1 *medium onion, cut into chunks*

1. Put all marinade ingredients in a blender and blend to a smooth sauce. If you do not have a blender, grate the onion and ginger, put the garlic through a press and stir everything together thoroughly.
2. Cut the chicken into quarters. Remove the neck, giblets, liver and wingtips and save to make stock.
3. Put the chicken quarters in a large glass, ceramic or stainless steel bowl. Cover with the marinade, making sure that each piece is well coated. Cover and refrigerate overnight.
4. Drain the chicken pieces and barbecue or grill until done. Use a medium low fire to avoid burning the chicken.
*Serves 4.*

## Skillet Chicken Italiano

Easy, quick, simple and delicious — it even reheats well!

2 *teaspoons oil*
1 *chicken* 3–4 *lbs., cut in serving pieces*
1 *large onion, sliced*

1 *cup sliced mushrooms (optional)*
1 16-*oz. jar or tin spaghetti sauce*

1. Rinse the chicken pieces with cold water. Pat dry.
2. Heat the oil in a skillet or frying pan. Brown the chicken pieces a few at a time. Set aside.
3. Pour off all oil. Return chicken to the skillet with the remaining ingredients. Cover and simmer 45 minutes or until chicken is tender. Serve with hot, cooked pasta.
*Serves 4.*

## Chicken Picatta (Italian)

With veal prices becoming astronomical, we found a truly easy substitute for veal picatta. For a real time saver, make a batch of chicken scallops (complete step 1), layer with waxed paper, wrap tightly and freeze. Remove a few as needed and cook *without* thawing — just cook a little slower.

| | |
|---|---|
| *breast meat from 2 chickens* | *2 tbs. lemon juice* |
| *whole-wheat flour* | *2 tbs. stock* |
| *salt and pepper* | *¼ cup parsley, chopped finely* |
| *2 tablespoons vegetable oil* | *1 teaspoon capers w/liquid* |
| *1 teaspoon grated lemon rind* | *(optional)* |

1. Cut chicken into pieces about 2½" square. Dip in flour. Place floured slices between sheets of waxed paper and pound lightly to make them "scallops." Dip scallops again in flour and sprinkle with salt and pepper.
2. Heat oil in a frying pan and brown scallops lightly on both sides. Add lemon rind, juice, stock and half the parsley. Cover and cook 7 minutes. Stir in the capers.
3. Arrange scallops on a warm platter and pour the lemon sauce over.
4. Garnish with lemon slices and parsley, if desired. *Serves 4.*

## Turkey Tetrazzini (Italian)

This is a terrific way to use up leftover turkey — but it's such a good dish that I often poach a turkey breast or thigh to make it. The sauce may be prepared in advance — complete Step 1. Refrigerate sauce until needed.

2 oz. butter
4 tablespoons oil
2 oz. whole-wheat flour
¼ pint hot milk
¼ pint hot turkey or chicken broth
salt and white pepper to taste
⅛ teaspoon nutmeg

¼ cup sherry
½ cup plain yogurt
1 oz. butter
½ lb. fresh mushrooms, sliced
2–3 cups diced cooked turkey
½ cup grated Parmesan cheese
hot, cooked whole-wheat spaghetti

1. Heat the 2 oz. butter and the oil. Blend in the whole-wheat flour and cook, stirring for about 2 minutes. Add the hot milk, then the broth. Stir over low heat until thickened. Add salt and pepper to taste; then the nutmeg and sherry. Remove from the heat and stir in the yogurt. Keep warm, over very low heat.
2. Heat the 1 oz. butter and sauté the mushrooms for about 5 minutes, or until soft. Toss the mushrooms and half of the sauce with the cooked spaghetti. Stir the diced turkey into the remaining sauce.
3. Arrange the spaghetti mixture in a ring on a large serving dish and pour the turkey and sauce in the centre. Top with cheese.
*Serves 6.*

## Viennese Duck with Sauerkraut Dressing

The tanginess of sauerkraut is a perfect match for crisp, roasted duck. The duck is roasted slowly to reduce fat. Accompany with dark bread and new potatoes.

DUCK
one or two 4–5 lb. ducklings, quartered

garlic
salt and pepper

1. Heat oven to 450°F.
2. Remove excess fat from ducks and prick the skin with a fork. Rub with cut garlic cloves and sprinkle with salt and pepper.
3. Place ducks, skin side down, in a large roasting pan and bake for 20 minutes. Drain off fat and set aside.
4. Reduce oven heat to 350°F. and bake 40–60 minutes more or until ducks are done. Turn the ducks occasionally as they cook.

DRESSING

½ cup duck fat
1 cup minced onion
1½ oz. whole-wheat flour
1¼ pints water or duck-giblet broth

1 teaspoon caraway seeds
1 teaspoon sweet paprika
2 lbs. sauerkraut, rinsed in cool water and drained

5. Heat the duck fat in a large pan and sauté the onion until golden. Stir in the flour. Gradually add the water or broth while stirring. Add the caraway seeds and paprika. Bring to a boil and cook for about 15 minutes to reduce the sauce to about ¾ pint. Add the sauerkraut and cook 5 minutes more.

*To serve:* Arrange the dressing on a large platter and arrange the pieces of duck on the dressing.

*Serves 4–8 (one quarter duck per serving).*

## Rabbit with Mustard Sauce (French)

A classic French dish using economical, low-fat rabbit. If you choose to substitute chicken, though, reduce the cooking time in Step 4 to about 25 minutes.

| | |
|---|---|
| 1 *rabbit, cut in serving pieces (chicken may be substituted)* | 1 *oz. whole-wheat flour* |
| | ½ *cup chicken stock* |
| | 1 *cup yogurt* |
| 1 *oz. butter* | 1 *cup half milk and half cream* |
| ¼ *cup brandy* | 2 *tablespoons minced parsley* |
| *Dijon-type mustard* | 10 *mushrooms, sliced* |
| 2 *tablespoons oil* | *lemon juice to taste* |
| 2 *spring onions* | |

1. Heat 1 oz. butter in a large frying pan. Add the rabbit pieces and sauté until browned. Add the brandy and ignite. When the flame subsides, remove the rabbit to a plate.
2. Smear the rabbit pieces on all sides with the mustard, more or less generously according to your taste.
3. Add the oil to the frying pan and stir the spring onions until limp. Add the flour and stir for a minute or two to cook the flour. Stir in the stock, yogurt, milk and cream.
4. Return the rabbit to the pan. Add the parsley and mushrooms. Cover loosely (cover should be slightly ajar) and simmer for 45 minutes, or until rabbit is done. Raise heat to high and stir 5 minutes.
5. Remove rabbit and continue to stir the sauce over high heat until it is thick. Add lemon juice to taste and serve the sauce over the rabbit.
   *Serves 4.*

## Rabbit Provençal (French)

The sunny flavour of Provençe is in this rich melange, garnished with olives. Chicken can be substituted if the cooking time in Step 4 is reduced to about 25 minutes.

1 *rabbit, cut up (chicken may be substituted)*
2 *rashers bacon, diced (optional)*
3–4 *tablespoons olive oil*
2 *medium onions, chopped*
4 *medium tomatoes, peeled, seeded and chopped*
2 *large cloves garlic, crushed*
1 *bay leaf*
1 *teaspoon minced parsley*
½ *teaspoon dried thyme*
¼ *pint white wine (dry)*
12–18 *stoned green olives (optional)*
*salt and pepper to taste*

1. Render the bacon in a large, heavy pan. When it is becoming crisp, remove it with a slotted spoon.
2. Add the oil, and brown the rabbit pieces, a few at a time. When the rabbit is browned, pour off all but about a tablespoon of fat.
3. Add the onions to the hot fat and stir them until they are wilted. Add the garlic.
4. Return the rabbit to the pan, and sprinkle over it the bacon, tomatoes, thyme, parsley, bay leaf, salt and pepper, and wine. Bring to a boil, cover, lower heat and simmer until done, about 45 minutes to an hour.
5. Remove the rabbit and tomatoes to a platter, and keep warm.
6. Heat the remaining sauce to a rolling boil and let it boil down until it is reduced by about ⅔. Stir it occasionally.
7. Stir the olives into the sauce to heat them, and pour the sauce over the rabbit. Very good with brown rice and sautéed aubergines.

*Serves 4.*

# Meats

## Yankee Pot Roast

This is so good that I make a larger roast, just to have some left over.

*about 2¼ lbs. silverside or bottom round of beef, without bones*
*whole-wheat flour*
*3 tablespoons oil*
*beef bones (see note)*
*3 cloves garlic, peeled and cracked*
*1 onion, in chunks*

*1 carrot, in chunks*
*¾ pint beef broth*
*½ teaspoon dry thyme*
*1 tablespoon fresh parsley*
*2 tbs. sherry*
*1 tablespoon Worcestershire sauce*
*salt and pepper to taste*

NOTE: Beef bones are optional, but they do add extra flavour and calcium to the sauce. Leftover bones may be used.

1. Flour the meat lightly. Heat the oil and brown the meat on all sides to seal juices. Remove it to a plate. Discard any remaining oil.
2. PRESSURE COOKER: Put meat, bones, vegetables and all remaining ingredients into cooker. Seal. Bring to pressure, cook 35 minutes. Let stand 5 minutes. Cool in cool water bath.
   STOVETOP: Put meat, bones, vegetables and all remaining ingredients into heavy pot. Cover tightly. Cook at simmer 1½ hours or until meat is tender.
3. Remove meat to a warm platter. Strain broth. (Remove and discard any bones). Place vegetables in a blender or food processor. Adding only enough sauce to make processing possible, purée the vegetables.

Return the purée to the remaining sauce and mix well.

4. If thickening is needed, bring the sauce to a boil and stir in 2 teaspoons cornflour *or* arrowroot mixed with 2 tbs. water. Stir until thickened.

5. Place the roast on a platter. Moisten with a little sauce. Serve the remaining sauce in a sauceboat.

   *Serves 4.*

As with most foods cooked in a seasoned liquid, pot roast reheats wonderfully. We like to prepare it through Step 2, chill it overnight (up to 3 days), and remove excess fat. Heat thoroughly before proceeding with Step 3.

## Rump Steak Rouladen (Germany)

Easy and economical.

| | |
|---|---|
| 1 *rump steak, about 1½ lbs. in one piece* | 2 *teaspoons Dijon mustard* |
| 1 *large onion, chopped* | 8 *cornichons or other tiny sour pickles (optional)* |
| 1 *cup fine, dry whole-wheat bread crumbs* | 1 *tablespoon oil* |
| 3 *fl. oz. water* | ½ *pint stock* |
| ¼ *cup chopped fresh parsley* | ¼ *pint red wine* |

1. Lightly score the steak on both sides and pound to flatten.

2. Mix together the onion, crumbs, water and parsley.

3. Smear one side of the steak with the mustard. Spread with the onion mixture. Arrange the cornichons in a row in the centre of the steak. Roll up, starting on a long side, and tie securely.

4. Heat the oil in a heavy frying pan and brown the meat on all sides. Transfer the browned meat to a heavy casserole or Dutch oven.

5. Add the stock and wine. Bring to a boil, cover and simmer 1 hour and 45 minutes or until meat is very tender.

6. Remove meat to a platter. Remove strings, keep warm.

7. Reduce cooking liquid by boiling rapidly until it is reduced by two-thirds. Serve over sliced meat roll.
*Makes 4–6 servings.*


## Cholent (Israel)

Rib-sticking and delicious meal-in-one-pot that cooks while you snooze.

9 *ozs. dried broad beans*
2 *tablespoons oil*
1 *piece beef brisket, about 2 lbs.*
¼ *cup chopped onion*
2 *cloves garlic, minced*
3 *oz. pearl barley*

4 *large potatoes, in 1″ cubes*
2 *large carrots, in 1″ chunks*
1 *large onion, in chunks*
1 *oz. whole-wheat flour*
2 *tablespoons soy sauce*
*salt and pepper to taste*

1. Soak the broad beans overnight in water to cover. Drain.
2. Heat the oil in a large pot or frying pan. Brown the brisket well on all sides. Add the chopped onion and the garlic and brown lightly. Remove the beef to a platter. Stir a little water into the pan to scrape up all the browned bits, onion and garlic. Pour over the meat.
3. Into a large slow cooker or ovenproof casserole, place the meat with its brown juices, the beans, barley, potatoes, carrots and onions. Sprinkle with whole-wheat flour. Add water to cover by one inch.
4. SLOW COOK at low temperature *OR* BAKE, covered at 350°F. for 4 hours.
*OR* SLOWBAKE in a 200°F. oven overnight.
5. Season to taste with soy sauce. Add salt and pepper to taste.

NOTE: Turnips or swedes are delicious in this dish. Vary the proportions of vegetables to suit your taste.
*Makes 5 generous servings.*

## Beef Stroganoff (Russian)

Fit for a Tsar, but easy to make.

| | |
|---|---|
| 1 *lb. tender steak (fillet, sir-loin)* | *dash freshly ground white pepper* |
| ½ *lb. mushrooms, sliced* | 1½ *oz. whole-wheat flour* |
| 1 *large onion, sliced thinly* | 8 *fl. oz. rich beef stock* |
| 1 *oz. butter* | ½ *teaspoon dry mustard* |
| 2 *tablespoons oil* | 1 *cup yogurt (sour cream may* |
| 1 *teaspoon salt* | *be used)* |

1. Slice the steak very thin and cut into strips about 2″ long.
2. Heat ½ oz. butter in a large, heavy frying pan and sauté the onion until it is translucent. Remove the onion with the slotted spoon and add the remaining butter. Sauté the mushrooms until they are becoming limp. Remove them with a slotted spoon and add them to the onions. Add the oil to the frying pan and sauté the steak until it is beginning to change colour. Sprinkle with salt and pepper, stir and remove with a slotted spoon. Add to the mushrooms and onions and keep warm.
3. To the oil remaining in the pan, add the flour and stir to mix until the flour is bubbly. Add the stock to the flour mixture. Stir and cook until the stock is thickened. Add a bit of stock to the dry mustard and stir until smooth. Add the mustard mixture to the sauce.
4. Return the onions, meat and mushrooms to the stock and heat through. Taste for seasoning. Remove from heat and stir in the yogurt. Serve with noodles or rice. *Serves 4.*

## Middle-Eastern Beef and Bean Stew

From the Middle East comes an unusual beef stew that is excellent with TABBOULEH. The original recipe had white beans but we like the flavour and extra nourishment of soybeans. As do all stews, this reheats very well.

| | |
|---|---|
| 6 *oz. cup dry soybeans* | 1 *bay leaf* |
| 3 *lbs. stewing beef* | 1½ *pints beef stock* |
| 3 *medium onions* | 4 *medium tomatoes* |
| 2 *tablespoons peanut oil* | ¼ *lb. raw brown rice* |
| 2 *teaspoons salt* | 1 *tablespoon lemon juice* |
| ¼ *teaspoon cinnamon* | |

Wash the soybeans and cover with cold water. Bring to a boil, remove from the heat and let them stand one hour. Drain the beans, cover with fresh cold water, bring to a boil and simmer over low heat one hour. Drain.

Trim the beef and cut it into 2-inch cubes. Cut the onions into chunks.

Heat the oil in a large, heavy pot. Brown the beef, a few pieces at a time. Remove the beef and sauté the onions until they begin to be translucent. Return the beef to the pot and add the beans, salt, cinnamon, bay leaf and ½ pint of the stock. Cover and simmer for 1¼ hours.

While the beef is simmering, drop the tomatoes into boiling water for about 15 seconds. The skins should peel off easily. Remove the seeds and chop the tomatoes coarsely.

Add the tomatoes, rice, lemon juice and 1 pint stock to the stew. Cover and simmer 45 minutes more or until the rice is done.

*Serves 6.*

## Boeuf Bourgignon (French)

A thoroughly elegant beef dish, which is actually just a superior stew.

THE STEW

| | |
|---|---|
| 2 *lbs. round or braising steak* | 4 *cloves garlic, minced* |
| *in ¾" cubes* | ¾ *pint red wine* |
| 1 *oz. whole-wheat flour* | 1 *tablespoon tomato paste* |
| 2 *tablespoons oil* | *Bouquet garni (thyme, parsley* |
| 1 *onion, chopped* | *& bay leaf)* |
| 1 *medium carrot, chopped* | ¼ *teaspoon white pepper* |

1. Sprinkle the steak with the whole-wheat flour. Shake off excess.
2. Heat the oil in a heavy pan. Add the meat and stir to brown. Add the onion, carrot and garlic. Mix well. Add half the wine and stir to scrape the browned bits from the bottom of the pot.
3. Stir in the remaining wine, tomato paste, *bouquet* and pepper. Bring to a boil, cover and simmer over low heat 1½ hours.*

\* At this point, dish may be chilled and reheated.

THE ACCOMPANIMENTS

1½ lbs. cooked, diced, unpeeled potatoes, preferably cooked in beef stock

1 lb. cooked small white onions

4–6 oz. small fresh mushrooms, quartered and sautéed

parsley to garnish

1. Stir the potatoes, onions and mushrooms into the hot stew and cook to heat through. Discard the *bouquet garni*.
2. Serve, garnished with parsley.
*Serves 4.*

## Spareribs with Sauerkraut (German)

2 lbs. pork spareribs, cut into serving-sized pieces

3 tablespoons oil

2 onions, cut up

1½ pints sauerkraut (home-made, if possible)

5–6 medium potatoes, in chunks

2 apples (cooking-type) cored and sliced

¼ pint white wine

salt and pepper to taste

Heat the oil and brown the ribs. Pour off excess oil. Stir the onions with the ribs until the onions are becoming translucent. Remove from heat.

Place a layer of ribs and onions in the bottom of a large pressure cooker (or dutch oven). Add a layer of sauerkraut, a layer of potatoes, and a layer of apples. Repeat the

layers until all of the ingredients are used. (Size of pot will determine the number of layers.) There should be some liquid from the sauerkraut. Add the wine to the pot, and if the liquid looks scant, add ½ cup water. Bring to a boil, cover and cook at 15 lbs. pressure for 15 minutes. (Or cover and simmer 1½ hours.) Adjust seasoning.
   *Serves 4 generously.*

## Beef-Rhubarb Stew (Mid-East)

As rhubarb is acid, it goes very nicely with meats.

| | |
|---|---|
| 2 *tablespoons oil* | ½ *cup chopped parsley* |
| 1 *lb. stewing beef in* ½″ *cubes* | ½ *pint water* |
| 1 *onion, chopped* | 12 *oz. rhubarb stalks in* 2″ |
| ½ *teaspoon salt* | *pieces & stewed without* |
| ½ *teaspoon white pepper* | *sugar* |
| ½ *teaspoon cinnamon* | 2 *teaspoons cornflour mixed* |
| ¼ *teaspoon nutmeg* | *with* 2 *tablespoons water* |

1. Heat the oil. Brown beef cubes on all sides. Add onion, salt, pepper, cinnamon, nutmeg, parsley and water. Bring to a boil.
2. Lower heat and simmer 1–1½ hours or until beef is tender.
3. Add rhubarb and cook 5 minutes longer.
4. Stir in cornflour and water mixture.
5. Serve with hot, cooked rice.
   *Serves 4.*

## Carbonnades à la Flamande (Belgian)

The Flemish beef stew is redolent with onions and flavoured with beer.

| | |
|---|---|
| *whole-wheat flour (about* ¼ *lb.)* | 1½ *lbs. lean stewing beef, cubed* |
| *salt and pepper* | 2 *tablespoons oil* |

1 *clove garlic, minced*
1 *cup beef stock*
5 *large onions, sliced*
1 *small tin beer*

1 *tablespoon Dijon mustard*
1 *tablespoon chopped parsley*
1 *bay leaf*
$\frac{1}{4}$ *teaspoon dried thyme*

1. Mix whole-wheat flour with salt and pepper to taste and dredge beef in it.
2. Heat the oil and brown the beef cubes, a few at a time.
3. Stir the garlic into the oil remaining in the pot. Stir in the beef stock, stirring up any browned bits.
4. Add a layer of beef to the pot, then a layer of onions, then beef, etc. until all are used up. Add all remaining ingredients.
5. PRESSURE COOKER: Cover, bring to pressure, cook 12 minutes.
   RANGETOP: Cover, cook at simmer $1\frac{1}{2}$ hours.
6. Serve with boiled new potatoes.
   *Serves 4.*

## Posole (Americas)

Make this hearty, spicy Mexican stew a few days ahead. It reheats very well.

$1\frac{1}{2}$ *lbs. meaty beef short ribs*
2 *tablespoons chili powder, or to taste*
$2\frac{1}{2}$ *pints water*
$\frac{1}{4}$ *cup vinegar*
$\frac{1}{2}$ *teaspoon salt*

1 *medium onion, finely chopped*
2 *cloves garlic, minced*
2 *teaspoons oregano*
2 *tins golden hominy, 15 oz. each, drained*

1. DAY BEFORE. Place the ribs, chili powder, water, vinegar and salt in a large pot. Bring to a boil, cover and simmer over low heat 4 hours. Allow to cool.
2. Remove all grease and fat. Chop or tear meat finely. Discard bones. Return meat to broth.

* If unavailable, substitute 1 cup diced raw potatoes and 1 cup drained, cooked corn in step 3.

3. Bring broth to a boil. Add all remaining ingredients.
   Cover and simmer 30  minutes.
   *Serves 4.*

## Meat and Cherry Stew (Mid-East)

Combining meat and fruit in surprising ways is a charac-
teristic of Middle Eastern cooking and produces delightful
results.

| | |
|---|---|
| 2 *tablespoons oil or clarified butter* | ½ *cup water* |
| 1 *lb. lean cubed lamb or beef* | ½ *stoned dark cherries (as sour as possible)* |
| 1 *large onion, minced* | 2 *tablespoons lime juice (about)* |
| ½ *teaspoon turmeric powder* | |
| ½ *teaspoon ground cinnamon* | *dash pepper* |

1. Heat the oil. Brown the lamb on all sides. Remove with
   a slotted spoon. Set aside.
2. Stir the onion into the oil remaining in the pan. Stir
   until it is becoming translucent. Add the turmeric and
   cinnamon and mix thoroughly.
3. Add the water. Stir vigorously with a wooden spoon to
   stir up all the browned bits. Return the meat and any
   accumulated juices. Cover and simmer 40 minutes.
4. Add the cherries and simmer, covered, 10 minutes.
   Taste.
5. Add lime juice and pepper to taste. The dish contains
   no salt and should be fairly tart.
6. Simmer, covered, 20 minutes more or until meat is
   tender.
   *Serves 4.*

## Marinated Beef Kebabs (Mid-East)

Simply one of the best kebab recipes we've ever found.

THE MEAT

1½ *lbs. beef round in* 1" *cubes*    ½ *teaspoon pepper*
*vegetable oil*    ½ *teaspoon oregano*
1 *teaspoon salt*

THE VEGETABLES (YOUR
CHOICE)

1 *green pepper, cut in chunks*    *small squash, cut in chunks*
*whole or quartered mushrooms*    *several pearl onions or yellow*
*several cherry tomatoes*      *onions cut in chunks*

GARNISH

1 *lemon*

1. In a non-porous glass container cover meat with oil, salt, pepper and oregano. Marinate overnight or at least 4 hours in refrigerator.
2. Alternate beef cubes on skewer with vegetables. Grill until beef is done to taste.
3. Place on bed of Rice Pilaf (p.   ), garnish with lemon wedges.
*Serves 4.*

## Italian Meat Loaf with Sauce

Complete this simple, inexpensive family favourite with hot pasta and a crisp salad.

MEAT LOAF

½ *cup bulgur wheat*    ¼ *cup minced fresh parsley*
1 *lb. lean minced beef*    1 *egg, lightly beaten*
1 *clove garlic, finely minced*    ½ *teaspoon dried oregano*
1 *oz. freshly grated Parmesan*    ½ *teaspoon salt*
   *cheese*    ¼ *teaspoon cayenne*

SAUCE

1 *medium onion, chopped*    ½ *cup red wine or stock or water*
2 *cups cooked or tinned toma-*    2 *cloves garlic, minced*
   *toes, undrained*    2 *tablespoons tomato paste*

1. Soak the bulgur wheat in 1 cup water for 20 minutes. Drain.

2. Heat oven to 375°F.
3. Crumble the mince into a large bowl. Using a fork, mix in the bulgur and remaining meat loaf ingredients. Mix thoroughly. Gently form into a loaf that will later fit loosely into a heatproof casserole.
4. Mix all ingredients for sauce. Place in the heatproof casserole and bring to a boil on top of the stove. Carefully slide in the loaf.
5. Place casserole, uncovered, into the oven and bake 45 minutes.
6. To serve, place the meatloaf on a large platter, surrounded with cooked pasta and top with the sauce. *Serves 4.*

## Picadillo (Americas)

Anywhere in South or Central America, you will find a version of picadillo. This versatile savoury concoction can top rice or noodles, fill a tortilla (or pitta bread), stuff a pepper or squash, or glamorize an omelet. We have had picadillo without tomatoes, without olives, mildly spiced, piquantly hot, and including chopped, hard-boiled eggs.

2 *tablespoons annatto oil (see p.    )*
1 *large onion, finely chopped*
4 *cloves garlic, minced*
2 *large green peppers, seeded and chopped fine*
3 *tinned jalapeno peppers, minced (2 fresh green chilis may be substituted)*

4 *medium tomatoes, peeled, seeded and chopped*
3 *oz. seedless raisins*
⅓ *cup pimiento stuffed olives, sliced*
¼ *teaspoon cumin powder*
⅛ *teaspoon clove powder*
2 *tablespoons cider vinegar*

1. Heat oil. Add meat and stir until no longer pink. Stir in all remaining ingredients and stir over moderate heat until the meat is cooked and very little liquid can be seen. Let cool or use hot.
*Makes 12 portions.*
Cooked picadillo will store in the refrigerator for about 4 days, and freezes very well.

## Swedish Meatballs

Excellent with noodles!

1 *large baking potato, cooked and skinned*
6 *tablespoons vegetable oil*
½ *cup minced onion*
1 *lb. lean minced beef*
¼ *cup bran*
¼ *cup fresh, fine pumpernickel breadcrumbs*
1 *egg, lightly beaten*

3 *tablespoons minced parsley*
½ *teaspoon ground allspice*
1 *teaspoon salt*
1½ *cups yogurt*
1 *oz. whole-wheat flour*
½ *cup stock or water*
1½ *tablespoons dried dill weed or ⅓ cup chopped fresh dill leaves*

1. Mash the potato very smooth.
2. Heat 2 tablespoons of the oil and sauté the onion until translucent. Add it to the potato. With a fork, stir in the beef, bran, crumbs, egg, parsley, allspice, salt and ½ cup of the yogurt. Beat until fluffy or combine in a food processor.
3. Oil a large shallow baking pan, using 2 tablespoons oil.
4. With 1 spoons, form meatballs and drop them onto the prepared pan. Make balls about 1½" and space about ½" apart on the pan. Make only as many balls as will fit in the pan and set the rest of the mixture aside. Grill the balls to brown lightly on all sides. Repeat until all the meat mixture has been cooked.
5. Add ½ cup yogurt to the baking pan and stir to scrape up all the browned bits. Set aside.
6. In a large saucepan, heat the remaining 2 tablespoons oil. Stir in the flour and when it is bubbling, stir in the stock, the remaining ½ cup yogurt and the yogurt from the baking pan. Stir until thickened. Add the meatballs and heat through.
7. Serve on a platter, garnished with dill.

NOTE: Meatballs can be made ahead through Step 6 and reheated.

*Serves 4.*

## Sauce Bolognese (Italian)

This is a marvellous meat and tomato sauce for any kind of pasta

1 *lb. minced beef*
½ *lb. Italian sausage\* (option-*
  *al), sliced ½"*
1 *tablespoon oil, if needed*
1 *onion, chopped*
1 *carrot, chopped*
1 *stalk celery, chopped*
1–3 *cloves garlic, minced*

½ *pint red wine*
1½ *pints tomato purée*
1 *teaspoon dried oregano*
1 *teaspoon dried basil*
4 *tablespoons tomato paste*
¼ *lb. mushrooms, sliced*
  *(optional)*

HINT: To save time, chop the onion, carrot, celery and garlic together in a food processor.

1. In a large, heavy pot, place the beef and sausage. Heat, stirring, until the pot is moderately hot and the meat is beginning to brown. At this point, if the meat is sticking, add about a tablespoonful of oil. Whether or not you'll need it will depend on how much fat is in the meat.
2. Stir in the vegetables. Continue to stir until the meat is browned. Add the wine and scrape up any browned bits still clinging to the pot.
3. Add all remaining ingredients. Mix thoroughly. Simmer 20 minutes.
   *Makes about 3 pints. Freezes well.*

NOTE: The secret to good Bolognese is *short* cooking. Longer simmering tends to make the tomatoes bitter.

\* Hot or sweet sausage may be used according to taste.

## Osso Buco

Veal shanks aren't always easy to find, but for *osso buco*, it's definitely worth it.

2 *tablespoons olive oil*
1 *medium onion, finely chop-*
  *ped*

1 *medium carrot, finely chop-*
  *ped*
2 *stalks celery, finely chopped*

2 *cloves garlic, minced*
1 *cup drained, tinned tomatoes,*
*chopped*
1 *tablespoon chopped fresh*
*basil (or 1 teaspoon dried)*
4 *lbs. meaty veal shanks cut in*
*3" chunks*
*whole-wheat flour*
*salt and pepper*

*oil*
2 *tablespoons fresh, chopped*
*parsley*
1 *teaspoon grated lemon rind*
½ *cup white wine (or stock)*
½ *cup stock*
1 *bay leaf*
*salt to taste*

1. Heat the 2 tablespoons olive oil in a very large, heavy casserole. Stir in the onion, carrot, celery and garlic and cook over very low heat until the vegetables are limp. Add the tomatoes and basil and cook, stirring, until the mixture is thick and quite dry. Set aside, away from heat.

2. Wash and dry the veal shanks. Mix the flour with a little salt and pepper. Roll the shanks in the seasoned flour and shake to remove excess flour. Heat the oil and brown the shanks on all sides, a few at a time. As the shanks are browned, transfer them to the casserole combining the vegetable mixture. Place shanks so that the marrow bone is upright.

3. When all of the shanks have been browned and transferred to the vegetable casserole, sprinkle them with the parsley, lemon rind, wine and stock. Add the bay leaf. Bring to a boil, cover the casserole very tightly and simmer over low heat for about an hour or until the meat is tender. Add a tablespoonful of stock from time to time if the liquid seems too low.

4. Transfer the cooked shanks to a warm platter, being careful not to lose the marrow.

5. Taste the sauce, add salt to taste, if needed. If sauce is too thin, cook, simmering, over high heat to reduce it. Pour some of the sauce over the meat, serve the rest in a sauceboat.

6. There are special Osso Buco spoons made to remove the marrow, but if you don't have them, improvise with anything narrow enough.

NOTE: Osso Buco may be made a day or two ahead and reheated. Reduce the sauce *after* reheating.
   *Serves 6.*


## Lemoned Lamb Roast (Mid-East)

Lemon and garlic add zip to roast leg of lamb.

1 *leg of lamb, about 4 lbs.*     *juice of 2 lemons*
4–5 *cloves garlic (or to taste)*    $\frac{1}{2}$ *teaspoon lemon zest*
*salt and pepper to taste*     $\frac{1}{2}$ *pint white wine*
2 *teaspoons dried oregano*

1. Trim lamb of fat.
2. Peel garlic and cut into thin slivers. With a sharp knife, stab slits into the fleshy part of the roast and insert garlic.
3. Sprinkle lamb on all sides with salt and pepper. Rub all over with the oregano. Place in a roasting dish and add the lemon juice, lemon zest and white wine.
   OPEN PAN METHOD: Place roast in a preheated 375°F. oven for 1 hour and 20 minutes (20 minutes per lb.) or until done to taste, basting occasionally.
   CLAY POT METHOD: Soak both halves of clay pot in water to cover for 15 minutes. Drain. Add lamb and other ingredients as above. Cover. Place in cold oven. Set heat at 480°F. Bake 75 minutes or until lamb is done to taste. Remove cover last 15 minutes to brown.
NOTE: A tasty sauce can be made by pouring the pan juices into a saucepan, adding stock to make $\frac{3}{4}$ pint liquid, bring to a boil and stir in 2 teaspoons arrowroot mixed with 4 teaspoons water. Cook and stir until thick.
   *Serves 6.*


## Hopi Lamb Stew (Americas)

Whether this dish is mild or fiery depends on how hot are the chilis used — it's good either way.

4 *juniper berries*
¾ *teaspoon coarse salt*
2 *cloves garlic, chopped*
1 *teaspoon dried oregano*
1 *lb. stewing lamb, in cubes*
2 *tablespoons whole-wheat flour*

2 *tablespoons oil*
1 *tin hominy (14½oz.) drained**
4 *long green chilis, peeled, seeded and chopped*
1 *medium onion, chopped*
3 *cups water*

* 2 cups diced raw potato may be substituted. Add 20 minutes before stew is done.

1. Crush the juniper berries, salt, garlic and oregano together in a mortar.
2. Toss lamb with the flour. Shake off excess.
3. Heat the oil and brown the lamb. Add the juniper mixture and all remaining ingredients. Bring to a boil. Skim. Cover and simmer 1¼ hours.
   *Serves 2–4.*
NOTE: This dish is more the consistency of a soup than a stew. The Hopi (a tribe of American Indians) serve it with lots of bread.

## Irish Stew

The authentic version — but it's also very good with a cup or two of green peas added in the last ten minutes of cooking.

4 *large potatoes, unpeeled, sliced ⅓" thick*
4 *large onions, peeled and sliced ⅓" thick*
3 *lbs. lamb chump chops*

1 *teaspoon salt*
½ *teaspoon freshly ground white pepper*
¼ *teaspoon thyme*

1. Lightly oil a heavy 8 pint casserole. Place half the potatoes in a layer in the casserole. Add half the onions and top with the lamb. Sprinkle with ½ teaspoon salt, ¼ teaspoon pepper and all of the thyme. Add the remaining onions and finish with the remaining potatoes. Sprinkle with the rest of the salt and pepper. Add

enough water to barely cover the potatoes.
2. Bring the casserole to a boil, cover, reduce the heat and simmer 1½ hours.
3. Serve with Irish soda bread and buttermilk (optional).
   *Serves 4.*

## Spanish Lamb Stew

Almonds and sherry impart the flavour of sunny Spain.

| | |
|---|---|
| 2 *tablespoons oil* | ¼ *teaspoon thyme* |
| 1 *large onion, chopped small* | ½ *cup water* |
| 1½ *lbs. lean lamb in 1″ cubes* | 4 *medium potatoes, diced* |
| 2 *cups tinned tomatoes* | ½ *cup raw or frozen peas* |
| ½ *cup whole almonds, toasted, then chopped or crushed finely* | 1 *tablespoon soy sauce* |
| | ½ *cup sherry (optional)* |
| | *salt and pepper to taste* |

1. Sauté the onion in the oil until translucent, add the lamb and stir until it is beginning to turn brown. Add the tomatoes, almonds, thyme and water. Cover the pot tightly and simmer gently ½ hour. Add water if needed.
2. Add the potatoes, cover the pot and simmer 20 more minutes.
3. Add the peas, soy sauce and the wine, cover and simmer 10 more minutes, or until done.
4. The sauce should be thick but water may be added as needed. Add salt and pepper to taste.
   *Serves 4.*

## Herbed Lamb Stew (Mid-East)

Versions of this wonderful dish can be found in nearly every part of the Mid-East as far east as Nepal and Pakistan.

1 *lb. lamb\* in ¾" cubes*
2 *tablespoons oil plus 2 tablespoons clarified butter or 4 tablespoons oil*
1 *medium onion, minced*
1 *teaspoon turmeric*
½ *pint water*
1 *tablespoon lime or lemon juice*

1 *cup minced spring onions*
1 *cup chopped spinach (one bunch)*
½ *cup chopped parsley*
¼ *cup chopped coriander leaves, if available*
1 *clove garlic, minced*
¾ *cup cooked black-eyed peas*
*salt and pepper to taste*

1. Heat oil and butter over medium heat and sauté onion until limp. Stir in turmeric.
2. Raise heat to moderately high. Add meat and stir to brown.
3. Reduce heat to medium. Add water and lime juice. Cover and simmer about 1 hour *or* until meat is tender.
4. Stir in spring onions, spinach, parsley, coriander, garlic and black-eyed peas. Cover and simmer 20 minutes more. Add salt and pepper to taste. Serve with rice.
   *Serves 4.*

NOTE: Chopping the spring onions, spinach, parsley and coriander is quick and easy in a food processor.
\* Beef may be substituted.

## Lamb-Tomato Stew

Excellent with Aubergine Purée

1 *lb. lean lamb in ½" cubes*
2 *tablespoons oil*
2 *medium onions, finely chopped*
½ *teaspoon turmeric*
4 *medium tomatoes, peeled, seeded and chopped*

*juice of 1 lime or lemon*
½ *cup water*
½ *teaspoon allspice powder*
2 *tablespoons chopped parsley*
2 *tablespoons chopped fresh coriander (cilantro)*
*salt and pepper to taste*

1. Heat the oil. Add the lamb and stir over moderate heat to brown. Add the onions and stir until the onions are becoming translucent. Stir in the turmeric.

2. Add the tomatoes, lime juice, water, allspice, parsley, coriander, and salt and pepper. Bring to a boil. Cover and simmer over low heat 1 hour or until meat is tender. Taste for seasoning.
*Serves 4.*

## Marinated Lamb Chops (Americas)

Try this for your next barbecue.

| | |
|---|---|
| *2 tbs. olive oil* | *½ teaspoon dried sage* |
| *2 tbs. vegetable oil* | *½ teaspoon powdered rosemary* |
| *3 tbs. lemon juice* | *⅛ teaspoon dried thyme* |
| *2 cloves garlic, crushed* | *⅛ teaspoon dried oregano* |
| *1 bay leaf* | *¼ teaspoon freshly ground pepper* |
| *1 teaspoon salt* | |
| *1 tablespoon chopped parsley* | *4–8 lamb chops (enough for four)* |

Mix all ingredients and add lamb chops. Marinate 6–12 hours. Grill, preferably over charcoal, until chops are done to taste. Baste with marinade as they cook.

## Indian Lamb on Skewers

Yogurt marinade makes the lamb melt-in-the-mouth tender.

| | |
|---|---|
| *2 lbs. lean lamb cut in 2″ cubes* | *1 teaspoon lemon juice* |
| *1 small onion* | *2 tablespoons grated fresh ginger (½ teaspoon powdered)* |
| *½ cup plain yogurt* | |
| *1 teaspoon ground cumin* | *2 cloves garlic, squished through a press* |

1. Chop the onion very fine and mix it with the yogurt, cumin, lemon juice, ginger and garlic. Add the lamb and toss to mix well.
2. Marinate overnight in the refrigerator or four hours at room temperature.

3. Drain the lamb.
4. Arrange the cubes on skewers and grill slowly until done.
   *Serves 4.*

## Lamb Shashlik (Mid-East)

Shish-Kebab at its very best!

2½ *lbs. lean lamb cubes (about*
   1½″ *square)*

MARINADE
2 *tbs. lemon juice*
2 *tbs. dry vermouth*
3 *tablespoons olive oil*
2 *teaspoons salt*
½ *teaspoon pepper*
2 *teaspoons dried oregano*
½ *teaspoons dried thyme*

½ *teaspoons dried rosemary*
4 *cloves garlic, minced*
*cherry tomatoes*
*red peppers*
*onions*
*mushrooms*
*lemon wedges*

1. Mix together the lemon juice, vermouth, oil, salt, pepper, herbs and garlic. Add the meat. Mix well. Marinate for at least 4 hours, mixing occasionally.
2. Remove the stems from the tomatoes. Seed the peppers and cut into 1½″ chunks. Cut the onions into chunks. Remove a small slice from the stem of each mushroom and cut into halves or leave whole, depending on size.
3. Alternate meat, tomatoes, peppers, onions and mushrooms on barbecue skewers. Grill until meat is done to taste. (Medium rare is best). Baste with any remaining marinade as shashlik is cooking. Serve hot with lemon wedges to season.
   *Serves 4.*

## Lamb Curry (India/Pakistan)

A quick and easy curry that's very good.

2 tablespoons oil

12 oz. lean lamb in ½″ cubes

1 medium onion, diced

2 teaspoons curry powder

1 cup parboiled broccoli florets

¼ pint stock

2 tbs. lemon juice

½ cup peas

1 tablespoon cornflour or arrowroot mixed with 2 tablespoons water

3 tablespoons plain yogurt

1. Heat the oil in a wok or frying pan. Add the lamb and stir until the lamb is lightly browned on all sides. Add onion and curry powder and stir until well mixed.
2. Add broccoli, stock and lemon juice. Mix well, bring to a boil, cover and simmer 5 minutes or until lamb is tender. Stir in the peas.
3. While stirring, slowly add the cornflour mixture. Simmer, stirring, until thick.
4. Remove mixture from heat. Stir in yogurt. Serve hot. *Serves 4.*

## Moussaka (Mid-East)

One of our favourite party casseroles because it can be mostly done ahead.

1 tablespoon peanut oil

4 medium onions, chopped

1½ lbs. minced lamb

3 tomatoes, peeled, seeded and chopped

½ cup dry red wine or stock

¼ teaspoon cinnamon

¼ cup chopped fresh parsley

2 oz. unsalted butter

1½ oz. whole-wheat flour

¾ pint warm milk

2 eggs, lightly beaten

1 cup cottage cheese, drained

2 medium aubergines

salt and pepper to taste

1 oz. whole-wheat bread crumbs

2 oz. grated Parmesan cheese

1. Heat the peanut oil in a large frying pan. Add the onions and stir until they become translucent. Add the meat and stir until it begins to brown. Add the tomatoes, wine or stock, cinnamon, parsley and salt to taste. Cook until nearly all the liquid is gone. Let cool.
NOTE: This part may be done a day ahead.

2. Melt the butter in a large, heavy pot. Add the flour and cook gently three minutes. Add the milk gradually, stirring. Cook five minutes, stirring occasionally. Remove from heat. Let cool a minute or two. Stir in the eggs, then the cottage cheese. Let cool.

NOTE: This may be done several hours ahead.

3. Peel the aubergines and slice about ¼″ thick. Steam the aubergine slices about 20 minutes or until tender.
4. Heat oven to 350°F.
5. Oil an oval sauteuse, baking dish or large casserole. Arrange a layer of aubergine in the bottom of the dish. Sprinkle with bread crumbs, Parmesan and some of the meat mixture. Repeat the layers until all the aubergine is used up (and all the meat mixture). Top with the cottage cheese mixture.
6. Bake one hour or until bubbly and slightly browned. Turn off the oven and let casserole sit in the cooling oven for one-half hour more.
*Serves 6.*

## Armenian Lamb Rissoles

A very different flavour for minced lamb. Beef would probably work well, too.

1 *lb. finely minced lean lamb*
½ *cup chopped fresh parsley*
½ *cup chopped onion*
2 *teaspoons salt*
¼ *teaspoon cayenne*

⅛ *teaspoon* each *cinnamon, nutmeg, cloves, ginger*
*whole-wheat flour*
2 *tablespoons vegetable oil*

1. Mix lamb with parsley, onion, salt, cayenne and spices. Knead thoroughly or mix in food processor until fairly smooth. Makes 4 patties.
2. Dip rissoles in flour to coat all sides.
3. Heat oil in a heavy frying pan. Cook rissoles over moderate heat until done to taste.
*Serves 4.*

## Keftethes — Greek Meat Balls

Mint makes these meatballs really special.

¾ *lb. minced lamb (or beef)*
2 *tablespoons bran*
2 *tablespoons dry whole-wheat bread crumbs*
1½ *tablespoon whole-wheat flour*
¼ *cup chopped fresh mint (2 tablespoons dry)*
½ *cup yogurt*
1 *large tomato, peeled, seeded and chopped*
5 *spring onions*
2 *tablespoons grated Parmesan cheese*
*parsley for garnish*

1. Place bran, bread crumbs, flour and mint in a large bowl. Stir in the yogurt. Let stand 10 minutes.
2. Mix in the meat, tomato, spring onions and cheese. Make 1½″ meatballs.
3. Grill the meatballs on a rack about 4 inches below the heat until brown, turning several times *or* brown on a rack in the centre of a convection oven. Garnish with parsley.

NOTE: May be made ahead and refrigerated or frozen. *Makes 24 meatballs (about).*

## Couscous (North African)

The first time you make couscous, it will seem like a lot of trouble, but your first taste will tell you it's worth it — and the variations are infinite (lamb only, chicken only, different vegetables, etc.). Besides, once you get the hang of it, you'll find couscous really easy. There is a vegetarian version on page

1 *lb. couscous (see glossary)*

THE STEW
¼ *cup oil*
2 *lbs. stewing lamb with bones*
2 *lb. stewing chicken, cut up*
*pinch of saffron*
½ *teaspoon ground turmeric*
2 *medium onions, in chunks*
1 *cinnamon stick*
1 *tablespoon chopped parsley*

4 tomatoes, peeled, seeded and chopped (1 large tin, drained)

*salt and pepper to taste*

LONG-COOKING
VEGETABLES
3–4 *carrots in* 1" *chunks*

3–4 *medium turnips or* 1 *lb swede, peeled, in* 1" *chunks*

SHORT-COOKING
VEGETABLES
1 *lb. courgettes or yellow squash in* 1" *chunks*
2 *cups cooked chickpeas, drained*

1 *cup fresh or frozen green peas*
2 *medium onions, in chunks*
4 *oz. dark raisins*

1. Heat the oil in the bottom of the couscousière or large pot. Brown meats, a few pieces at a time. Drain the oil and discard. Return all of the browned meat to the pot. Add the remaining stew ingredients and 4½ pints of water. Bring to a boil, cover and simmer 1 hour.
2. While the stew simmers, place the couscous in a large bowl and pour 4 pints cool water over it. Stir with your fingers, then drain off the water through a sieve. Return the couscous to the bowl and let stand 10 minutes. Rub couscous between dampened palms to separate grains and remove lumps. Cover with a damp cloth. Continue to step 3 when step 1 is complete.
3. Dampen a cloth and twist it securely around the outer rim of the steamer for the couscous. Adjust the steamer firmly over the simmering stew. (For a couscousière, a strip of damp cheesecloth should be sufficient). Slowly sprinkle the couscous into the steamer. Steam, uncovered, over the simmering broth for 20 minutes.
4. Remove the couscous steamer and dump the couscous onto a large tray or platter. Sprinkle it with ½ cup of cold water and a little salt. Stir well. Oil your hands and rub the couscous between the palms for a few minutes. Smooth the couscous and let it dry for 10 minutes. NOTE: At this point you may, if you wish,

take the meat from the pot and remove and discard the bones.

5. Add the long-cooking vegetables to the pot and let simmer 10 minutes. NOTE: At this point you may set the stew aside, cover couscous with a damp cloth, and everything will wait several hours.

6. Add the short-cooking vegetables to the simmering stew. Repeat step 3.

7. Dump the couscous into a large serving platter. Make a large well in the centre. Using a perforated spoon, fill the well with the meats and vegetables from the stew. Taste the broth and adjust seasoning if necessary. Strain the broth and pour a little over the grain. Serve extra sauce in a sauceboat.

*Serves 6.*

# Beans, Grains & Pasta

## Meatless Chili (Americas)

Making chili from soybeans, lentils and sesame seeds may not be traditional — but it sure is good!

| | |
|---|---|
| 6 *oz. dried soybeans* | 2 *tablespoons peanut oil* |
| 6 *oz. lentils* | 2 *tablespoons chili powder* |
| ½ *cup sesame seeds* | 4–6 *cloves garlic, chopped* |
| 2 *peppers* | ½ *teaspoon powdered cumin* |
| 3 *medium onions* | 2 *tablespoons soy sauce* |

1. Wash soybeans and cover with cold water. Bring to a boil, remove from heat and let stand one hour. Drain beans, cover with fresh, cold water, bring to a boil and simmer over low heat one hour. Drain. Reserve liquid.
2. Place the lentils and sesame seeds in a large pot with water to cover, including the liquid from the soybeans. Bring to a simmer.
3. Heat peanut oil. Chop peppers and onions finely and sauté them briefly, until barely limp. Add them with oil to lentils. Add soybeans, chili powder, garlic and cumin. Let simmer for about 60 minutes, or until everything is tender. Add more water if needed. Add soy sauce.
   *Serves 4 to 6.*

## Chili Beans (Americas)

The secret ingredient in this recipe is blackstrap molasses. The hint of smokey sweetness makes these beans truly extraordinary.

| | |
|---|---|
| 6 *oz. dried red beans* | 1 *tablespoon chili powder* |
| ¾ *pint water* | 2 *teaspoons blackstrap molas-* |
| 1 *tablespoon oil* | *ses* |
| 1 *medium onion, chopped* | 1 *teaspoon oregano* |
| 1 *clove garlic, chopped* | ½ *teaspoon cumin* |
| 1 *pepper, chopped* | |
| 16 *oz. tinned tomatoes, un-* | |
| *drained* | |

1. RANGETOP: Soak beans overnight. Cook 1 hour. Add remaining ingredients. Cook 1 hour.
   PRESSURE COOKER: Place beans, water and oil in cooker. Bring to pressure. Remove from heat immediately and let pressure reduce naturally.
2. Add all remaining ingredients to beans. Bring to pressure. Cook 5 minutes. Let cool 5 minutes. Reduce pressure quickly.
3. If desired, stir beans over moderate heat a few minutes to reduce liquid.
   *Serves 4.*

## Tostadas Compuestas (Mexico)

With beans, tortillas, cheese, fresh vegetables, guacamole and salsa, Tostadas Compuestas are a one-dish complete meal. For a buffet, let guests make their own combinations.

| | |
|---|---|
| 1 *tin tortillas, fried briefly until crisp** | 2 *cups Meatless Chili or Chili Beans* |

TOPPINGS

| | |
|---|---|
| 2 *oz. onion, chopped* | 1 *tomato, peeled and chopped* |
| 4 *oz. lettuce, shredded* | 4 *oz. grated sharp cheese* |

Layer tortillas with chili and toppings (or fill taco shells). Add a dollop of guacamole and season with Salsa Cruda to taste.

## Guacamole

1 *large or 2 small avocados, peeled and seeded*
2 *oz. tinned, finely chopped green chilis*
1 *tablespoon finely chopped on- ions*

2 *tablespoons lemon juice*
1 *teaspoon fresh coriander leaves (if available)*
2 *cloves garlic, crushed*

Mash the avocado and mix in all the remaining ingredients.

## Salsa Cruda ('Raw Sauce')

2 *oz. tinned, finely chopped green chilis*
2 *tomatoes, peeled, seeded and chopped fine*

2 *tbs. finely chopped onion*
1 *tablespoon cider vinegar*
3 *tablespoons chopped fresh coriander leaves*

Mix all ingredients and let stand at least 30 minutes before serving.

\* taco shells may be substituted

## Frijoles Negros

1 *lb. black (turtle) beans, soaked*
1 *green pepper, chopped*
1 *onion, chopped*

2 *cloves garlic, chopped finely*
1 *teaspoon oregano*
1 *bay leaf*

SOFRITO
1 *onion, chopped*
1 *green pepper, chopped*
1 *clove garlic, chopped*

2 *tablespoons vegetable oil*
1 *teaspoon olive oil*
$\frac{1}{4}$ *cup vinegar*
*salt to taste*

Add to the soaked beans the green pepper, onion, cloves garlic, the oregano and bay leaf. Add water according to the bean-cooking directions (page 178) and cook the beans until done.

Heat the oils and add the *sofrito* onion, pepper and garlic. Cook over moderate heat until the onion is wilted. Add the cooked *sofrito* and the vinegar to the cooked beans. Add salt to taste.

Serve the beans hot, with hot rice to accompany. Chopped fresh coriander leaves make a nice garnish.

*Serves 4–6 as a main dish.*

## Lentil Curry with Eggs (India/Pakistan)

A simple one-dish meal that needs only a frisky green salad for accompaniment.

6 *oz. lentils*
¾ *pint water*
½ *teaspoon salt*
4 *hard boiled eggs*
2 *tablespoons sesame oil*
2 *medium onions, chopped*
1 *tablespoon Indian curry powder*

2 *tablespoons lemon juice*
2 *peeled, seeded and chopped tomatoes*
5 *tablespoons plain yogurt*
*chopped spring onion*

1. Wash lentils carefully. Cook in water, with salt added, about 40 minutes or until tender.
2. Peel and halve hard boiled eggs.
3. Heat oil and cook onions until transparent. Add curry powder, lemon juice and tomatoes and cook until sauce is beginning to thicken. Stir in yogurt.
4. Stir most of yogurt sauce into hot lentils, reserving a few tablespoonfuls for garnishing. Arrange lentil mixture in dish and arrange egg halves, cut side up, on top of lentils. Top with the remaining sauce. Garnish with spring onion.

*Serves 4.*

NOTE: In India, this would be served at room temperature but if you'd like the eggs hot, shell them, and let them rest in a bowl of hot water until the lentils and sauce are done. Remove from the water, halve them and proceed.

## Spiced Golden Lentils (India/Pakistan)

Lentils are ubiquitous in Indian and Pakistani cuisine. Here's one of the tasty reasons why.

| | |
|---|---|
| 6 *oz. lentils* | 3 *tablespoons sesame oil* |
| $\frac{3}{4}$ *pint water* | 2 *medium, thinly sliced onions* |
| $\frac{1}{2}$ *teaspoon turmeric* | $\frac{1}{2}$ *teaspoon powdered cumin* |
| $\frac{1}{8}$ *teaspoon cayenne* | 3 *tablespoons lemon juice* |

1. Wash and pick over lentils as they often include small stones and lumps of clay.
2. Bring water to boil, add lentils, turmeric and cayenne. Simmer covered, about 30 minutes or until tender but not mushy.
3. Heat sesame oil, sauté onions until transparent and very limp. Stir onions and oil into cooked lentils. Add cumin and lemon juice and mix well.
   *Serves 4.*

## Lentils with Dried Fruit (Mid-East)

An unusual but delightful combination.

| | |
|---|---|
| 1$\frac{1}{2}$ *pints tinned tomatoes* | 12 *oz. lentils* |
| 3 *slices dried apple, in* 1″ *chunks** | 1$\frac{1}{2}$ *pints water* |
| | 2 *tablespoons olive oil* |
| 2 *slices dried pineapple, in* 1″ *chunks** | 1 *large onion, chopped* |
| | 2 *cloves garlic, minced* |
| $\frac{1}{3}$ *cup dried apricots, cut up** | 3 *teaspoons salt* |

1. Simmer the tomatoes and fruits together for about 45 minutes or until thickened.
2. Put the lentils in the water, bring to a boil, cover the pot and simmer for about 20 minutes, or until the lentils are tender.

3. Heat the olive oil in a frying pan. Add the onions and garlic, and sauté, stirring, until the onions are soft and translucent.
4. Add the tomato mixture, the onion mixture and the salt to the lentils, and stir to mix well. Simmer 10 minutes to blend the flavours.
*Serves 4.*

\* or use any dried fruits to total about ⅔ cup.

## Fagioli Napolitano

This is a delicious dish from Naples, which combines beautifully with pasta.

| | |
|---|---|
| 1 *cup cooked haricot beans* | 1½ *pints home-bottled tomatoes* |
| *(Navy beans will do)* | 1 *teaspoon oregano* |
| 2 *tablespoons olive oil* | 2 *teaspoons chopped parsley* |
| 2 *tablespoons vegetable oil* | 3–4 *sprigs fresh basil (if* |
| 2 *cloves garlic, cracked* | *possible)* |

1. Heat the oil in a small frying pan. Add the garlic. When the garlic is browned, remove and discard it. Remove the oil from heat.
2. Put the tomatoes in a large, heavy pot. Add the oregano, parsley and the oil. Stir. Cook over moderate heat, stirring occasionally, for about 40 minutes, or until the sauce is quite thick. Add the beans, and simmer for 10 minutes more. Garnish with the basil.
*Serves 4 as a side dish.*

## Fagioli Napolitano with Pasta

| | |
|---|---|
| ½ *lb. whole-wheat pasta, pre-* | 1 *recipe Fagiolo Napolitano* |
| *ferably elbow macaroni* | |

Cook the pasta in boiling, salted water until it is just cooked *al dente*. Add the drained pasta to the completed Fagioli Napolitano, and cook the mixture for about 5 minutes.
*Serves 4 as a main dish.*

## Chickpea Cakes (Greek)

A Greek tradition that's very different and very good.

3 *cups cooked chickpeas*
1 *medium onion, cut in chunks*
1 *cup cold, diced, boiled potato*
   *(do not peel)*
2 *cloves garlic*
1 *teaspoon lemon juice*

*salt and pepper to taste*
1 *egg, lightly beaten*
½ *cup chopped fresh parsley*
*olive oil or other vegetable oil*
*lemon wedges*
*parsley to garnish*

1. Mince the chickpeas, onion, potato and garlic in a mincer or food processor. Add lemon juice. Add salt and pepper to taste.
2. Stir in the egg and parsley.
3. Heat the oil in a large frying pan or on a griddle. When hot, drop chickpea mixture by tablespoonfuls. Cook slowly until brown on both sides, turning several times.
4. Serve hot, accompanied by lemon wedges and parsley garnish.
*Serves 4.*

## Chickpea Stew with Greens (Mid-East)

Because this dish is good hot or cold, it's super for a buffet, party or picnic.

3 *oz. dry chickpeas*
1 *tablespoon oil*
1 *bunch greens (about 1 lb.)*
   *spring greens, chard, spi-*
   *nach*

1 *large onion, chopped*
2 *cloves garlic, minced*
2 *tbs. tomato paste*
*dash cayenne*
2 *tbs. lemon juice*

RANGETOP: Soak the chickpeas overnight in water to cover. Add water to cover by 1 inch. Bring to a boil, simmer 2 hours or until tender, adding water as necessary. There should not be too much liquid. Add all remaining ingredients. Cover and simmer 20 to 30 minutes, or until greens are tender.
PRESSURE COOKER: Place chickpeas, ¾ pint water

and oil in pressure cooker. Cover, bring to pressure. Turn off, let cool. Add all remaining ingredients. Bring to pressure, cook 5 minutes, let cool 5 minutes then cool quickly.

*To Serve:* Good hot or cold, garnished with lemon wedges and cayenne or hot pepper sauce.

*Serves 4.*

## Soybeans Orientale

| | |
|---|---|
| 2 *tablespoons vegetable oil* | $\frac{1}{4}$ *cup soy sauce* |
| 4 *slices fresh ginger root* | 2 *cups cooked soybeans* |
| 1 *stalk celery, thinly sliced* | $\frac{1}{2}$ *cup sherry or stock* |
| 1 *carrot, thinly sliced* | 1 *cup fresh mung bean sprouts* |
| 1 *onion, quartered and sliced* |    *(optional)* |
| 2 *cloves garlic, crushed* | |

Heat the oil in a wok or large frying pan. Add the ginger and stir for a minute. Add the celery, carrot and onion and stir until the vegetables are just beginning to wilt. Add the garlic, stir, then add the soy sauce, soybeans and sherry. Cover the pot and simmer over low heat for 10 minutes. Remove the cover and raise the heat for a minute to reduce the sauce. Stir in the sprouts. Serve hot.

*Serves 4–6.*

## Felafel Sandwiches (Mid- East)

This super-healthy variation on the popular felafel and pita sandwich requires planning 4 or 5 days ahead, but it's worth it!

FELAFELS

| | |
|---|---|
| 6 *oz. dried garbanzo beans* | $\frac{1}{4}$ *teaspoon cumin* |
|    *(chick peas)* | 1 *tablespoon lemon juice* |
| 2 *cloves garlic, minced* | $\frac{1}{2}$ *tsp. salt* |
| 2 *tablespoons fresh parsley or* | *fine dry whole-wheat bread* |
|    *coriander leaves, chopped* |    *crumbs, about $\frac{1}{2}$ cup* |

Soak the garbanzo beans overnight. Sprout 3 or 4 days or until sprouts are about $\frac{1}{2}''$ long. In a food processor or blender, grind together the beans, garlic, parsley, cumin, tahini, cayenne, lemon juice and salt, (or mince the beans in a mincer and mix with the other ingredients.) Form balls about 1″ in diameter. Roll them in the bread crumbs.

Place the felafels on a baking sheet and bake at 350°F. for 25 minutes, turning twice.

DRESSING

1–3 *cloves garlic, finely minced*
4 *tablespoons lemon juice*

3 *tablespoons tahini (or enough to make a thick dressing)*
*pinch each cayenne and cumin*

Mix all ingredients thoroughly.

SANDWICHES

*whole-wheat pita bread*
1 *small cucumber (4 oz.) finely chopped*
1 *medium tomato, peeled, seeded and chopped*

4 *spring onions, minced*
2 *oz. alfalfa or mixed sprouts*
*plain yogurt*

*To assemble:*

Mix the dressing with the cucumber, tomato, spring onions and alfalfa sprouts.

Cut each pita in half. Place a spoonful of the vegetables in the pocket. Top with hot felafels. Lavish with yogurt.
*Serves 4*

## Meatless Dolmades (Middle Eastern Stuffed Grape Leaves)

Versatile Dolmades are good as a main dish, hors d'oeuvres or for a buffet. Tuck a few in a lunchbox.

1 *cup cooked kasha** (buck-wheat groats)
1 *cup cooked yellow split peas**
2½ *cups cooked brown rice*
1 *tablespoon oil*
1 *medium onion, chopped*
2 *teaspoons dried mint leaves*
1 *teaspoon dried dill weed*

1 *tablespoon tomato paste*
2 *tablespoons fresh lemon juice*
*salt and pepper to taste*
1 *one-pound jar grape leaves in brine*
8 *fl. oz. water with 2 table-spoons lemon juice*

1. Mix together the cooked kasha, peas and rice.
2. Heat the oil and sauté the onion until soft. Add to kasha mix.
3. Stir mint, dill, tomato paste, lemon juice, salt and pepper into kasha mix.
4. Rinse grape leaves in hot water. Remove stems.
5. With dull side of grape leaf toward you, place about a tablespoonful of filling at the stem end and roll once to cover filling. Tuck the side portions of the leaf over filling and roll up entire leaf. Continue until all filling is used.
6. Line large, heavy pot with leftover leaves. Cover with filled leaves, seam side down. Top with leftover leaves. Pour on the water-lemon juice mixture. Put a plate on top of all. Cover and simmer 1 hour over low heat. Serve hot, cold or room temperature.

*Makes about 50 dolmades*

* ½ cup dry product cooked in 1½ cups water 15–20 minutes.

## Stuffed Cabbage Rolls (Mid-East)

A hearty combination of vegetable, grain, pulses and spice.

24 *cabbage leaves*
¾ *pint water from cooking cabbage and/or chickpeas*

2 *tbs. lemon juice*

STUFFING

2 *tablespoons peanut oil*
1 *large onion, chopped*
1 *cup cooked chickpeas*
1 *cup cooked brown rice*
½ *cup chopped fresh parsley*
3 *tablespoons tomato paste*

½ *cup stock or cooking water*
½ *teaspoon allspice*
½ *teaspoon dried mint*
¼ *teaspoon garlic powder*
*salt and pepper to taste*

1. Heat the peanut oil and sauté the onion until soft. Place in a large bowl and mix in all the remaining stuffing ingredients.
2. Drop the cabbage leaves into boiling water until the colour brightens. Remove with tongs or a slotted spoon and rinse with cold water. Remove the tough centre rib.
3. Lay the cabbage leaves flat with the inside of the leaf facing you. Place a portion of the filling on each leaf and roll up, tucking the sides over the filling.
4. Line a large pot with any torn or discarded cabbage leaves. Arrange the stuffed rolls on top, seam side down. Sprinkle the rolls with the cooking water and the lemon juice. Cover with a plate to weigh down the rolls. The plate need not reach to the edges of the pot, but should sit directly upon the rolls.
5. Cover with a tight lid. Simmer 45 minutes. Let stand ½ hour before serving.
Serve warm or cold.
*Serves 6.*

## Steamed Millet

Although a staple grain in some parts of the world, we mostly know millet as birdseed. Give this delicious grain a try!

| | |
|---|---|
| 2 *tablespoon butter or oil* | 1¼ *pints stock* |
| 1 *tablespoon minced onion* | *salt to taste* |
| 6 *oz. whole millet* | |

Heat the butter or oil and sauté the onion until translucent. Add the millet and stir until shiny. Add the stock. Bring to a boil, cover and simmer over very low heat 30 minutes or until water is absorbed and millet is tender. Toss with a fork and add salt to taste. .

## Bulghur Pilaf (Russian)

Bulghur is cracked, partly cooked wheat, which makes a great, high-fibre pilaf.

| | |
|---|---|
| 2 *tablespoons oil* | 12 *oz. bulgur* |
| 1 *medium onion, chopped* | 1½ *pints hot chicken stock* |
| 1 *clove garlic, chopped* | 4 *tbs. lemon juice* |
| 2 *tablespoons chopped parsley* | |

Heat the oil and stir in the onion and garlic until translucent. Add the parsley and bulghur and stir until the bulghur is glistening. Add the stock and juice. Bring to a boil, cover and simmer for 20 minutes, or until bulghur is tender. Let stand off heat for 5 minutes more. Fluff with a fork. Serve hot.
*Serves 4.*

## Kasha (Russian)

The earthy, nutty flavour of kasha makes it a family favourite.

| | |
|---|---|
| 1 *egg* | 2 *tablespoons oil* |
| 6 *oz. kasha (buckwheat groats)* | 1 *medium onion, finely chopped* |
| ¾ *pint boiling water* | *salt and pepper to taste* |

1. Mix the egg with the kasha in a heavy pot (*not* glass or

enamelled). Over low heat, stir the kasha mixture until dry. Add the boiling water and cook the kasha over gentle heat until the water has all been absorbed. The kasha should be just tender. You may add a little more water if it is needed. Keep the kasha warm.

2. Heat the oil and sauté the onion until it is translucent. Toss the oil and onion with the kasha. Season to taste. *Serves 4.*

## Kasha Pilaf (Mid-East)

Hearty kasha is delicious in pilaf.

| | |
|---|---|
| 1 *tablespoon oil* | 2 *cloves garlic, chopped* |
| 1 *onion, chopped* | 6 *oz. whole kasha* |
| 1 *stalk celery, chopped* | 1½ *pints stock* |
| 1 *green pepper, chopped* | 3 *tablespoons soy sauce* |

Heat the oil in a large, heavy pot and sauté the onion, celery, pepper and garlic until onion is limp. Stir in the kasha until coated with oil. Add the stock and soy sauce. Bring to a boil, cover and simmer over low heat 20 minutes.
*Serves 4.*

## Polenta (Italian)

Italian corn meal mush — used like bread or potatoes.

| | |
|---|---|
| ½ *lb. finely ground yellow corn meal* | 1½ *pints boiling water* |
| | 1 *teaspoon salt* |

Stir the corn meal into the boiling water. Add the salt and stir over lowest heat for about 45 minutes or until the polenta is a near-solid mass. Turn out onto a plate and serve with butter and cheese, honey, tomato sauce, or whatever you like.
*Serves 4.*

## Fried Polenta

Cook the polenta as above. Turn it into a small, oiled loaf tin and let set until cooled. Turn it out of the tin, slice and fry in a little oil over low heat until crusty and golden, turning once. Serve with molasses.

## Tarhonya (Hungarian)

Tarhonya is really a dried pasta. A *must* with Chicken Hongroise.

| | |
|---|---|
| 1 *lb. whole-wheat flour* | 3 *eggs* |
| 1 *teaspoon salt* | |

Make a well in the centre of the flour and stir in the eggs and salt. Knead to make a smooth, elastic dough. Roll the dough as thin as possible, and cut into $\frac{1}{8}$ inch strips. Chop strips until the bits of dough are as fine as barley. Spread on baking sheets and dry in 150°F. oven for about 1 hour. Store in tightly covered container.

TO COOK

| | |
|---|---|
| 1 *med. onion, chopped* | 1 *cup tarhonya* |
| 2 *tablespoons vegetable oil* | 1$\frac{1}{4}$ *pints stock or water* |

Heat the oil and sauté the onion until golden. Add the tarhonya and stir to coat with oil. Add the stock, bring to a boil, and cook at simmer until all the stock is absorbed (about 20 minutes.) Season to taste.

*Serves 4.*

## Pasta Jardiniere (Italian)

Vary the vegetables to suit the season.

| | |
|---|---|
| 8 *oz. broccoli* | 1 *lb. sesame pasta (or other* |
| 1 *cup fresh peas (or frozen)* | *whole-grain pasta)* |
| 1 *small courgette (about 6 oz.)* | $\frac{1}{2}$ *cup ricotta cheese* |

½ *cup yogurt*
3 *spring onions, chopped*
2 *tablespoons chopped parsley*

2 *tablespoons grated Parmesan*
   *cheese*

SAUCE
1 *oz. butter*
2 *cloves garlic, crushed*
1 *oz. whole-wheat flour*

8 *fl. oz. stock (including water*
   *from steaming vegetables)*
¼ *teaspoon crushed red pepper*
   *(optional)*

1. Slice the broccoli stem very thin and break the top into florets. Steam over boiling water until barely tender. Remove, reserving the water. Rinse the broccoli briefly with cold water. Drain and set aside.
2. Steam the peas over the broccoli cooking water. Remove, reserving the water. Rinse the peas with cold water and set aside.
3. Slice the courgette very thin and steam as above. Measure the reserved water and add enough stock or water to make 8 fl. oz.
4. Heat a large quantity of fresh water to boiling. Add the pasta. Stir and allow to simmer about 10 minutes or until pasta is *al dente*.
5. While the pasta is cooking, make the sauce. Melt the butter in a large saucepan over moderate heat. Sauté the garlic, but do not allow it to brown. Add the flour and cook, stirring until the flour is bubbly. Stir in the stock and pepper until the sauce is thickened. Add the vegetables and heat thoroughly. Remove from heat and set aside.
6. Drain the pasta, reserving the water for cooking. Toss the drained pasta with the ricotta and yogurt to mix thoroughly. Add the vegetables and sauce and toss lightly. Top with the spring onions, parsley, and Parmesan.

*Serves 4.*

## Herbed Pasta (Italian)

A quick, easy change-of-pace dish made with very simple
ingredients.

1   *lb. whole-wheat pasta,*
    *cooked and drained*

HERB TOPPING

1 *oz. butter*

2 *tablespoons olive oil*

4 *spring onions, chopped finely*

4 *cloves garlic, crushed*

4 *tablespoons chopped parsley*

$\frac{1}{4}$ *pint sherry*

*salt and pepper to taste*

While the pasta is cooking, heat the butter and oil and
sauté the spring onions, garlic and parsley until limp. Do
not allow the garlic to brown. Stir in the sherry and season
to taste. Toss the sauce with hot, cooked drained pasta.
   *Serves 4.*


## Pasta E Finocchiella
*(Noodles with Fennel)*

1 *lb. bulb fennel*

*salt*

*spinach pasta (enough for
    four)*

*freshly grated Parmesan cheese*

Wash and trim the fennel. Cut the bulbs in half lengthwise
if they are small; quarter them, if large. Put fennel in a pot
with water to cover and salt to taste. Bring to a boil and
simmer until the fennel is tender. Remove the fennel from
the pot, reserving the liquid. Bring the liquid again to the
boil and add the pasta. Cook until done to taste. While the
pasta is cooking, shred the fennel finely. When the pasta is
cooked, drain. (Reserve the liquid for soup stock.) Toss
the cooked pasta with the shredded fennel, and sprinkle
generously with the cheese.
   *Serves 4.*

# Rice

Rice has been cultivated in Thailand since at least 3,500 B.C., spreading from there to India and China.

Moors introduced rice to Spain (Andulusia) in the 8th century A.D. Italy, now Europe's largest producer, began cultivating rice in the 10th century A.D., and it was introduced to the American Colonies in 1695.

Asia produces over 90% of the world's rice.

Rice is the staple grain (and often the major food) of 60% of the world's population.

Nearly all rice grown is used for human consumption unlike corn of which the bulk is used for animal feed.

Indian actress and cookbook author Madhur Jaffrey calls rice "quite addictive . . . It seduces without ever having to exert itself."

Brown rice is rice with only the husk removed.

White rice has the nutritious brown coating removed by milling.

Converted or "Easy Cook" rice has been parboiled to remove surface starch.

Enriched rice has a few of the vitamins lost in milling added back. If rice is washed, they are lost again.

Unopened packets of rice should be stored at cool room temperature. After opening, transfer the rice to a clean, dry jar with a tight lid. If you're going to store it for a long period, add a bay leaf to repel invaders.

RICE NUTRITION[1]

| 3 ounces | Calories | Protein g | Fat g | Carb. g | Crude Fibre | Dietary Fibre | Calcium mg |
|---|---|---|---|---|---|---|---|
| Cooked brown rice | 104 | 2.2 | 0.5 | 22.3 | 0.26 g | * | 11 |
| Cooked white enriched rice | 112 | 2.0 | 0.1 | 24.9 | 0.10 g | 7.09 g | 10 |

| 3 ounces | Phos. mg | Potas- sium mg | Thia- mine mg | Ribofla- vin mg | Niacin mg | B6 mg | Folacin mcg |
|---|---|---|---|---|---|---|---|
| Cooked brown rice | 64 | 61 | .08 | .02 | 1.2 | .16 | 14 |
| Cooked white enriched white | 29 | 29 | .11 | .07 | 1 | .05 | 16 |

\* Based on white rice figures,dietary fibre in brown rice could be as much as 18.2g.

[1] From *Nutrients In Foods, Leveille et al.*, Nutrition Guild, Cambridge, MA, 1983.

# Cooking Rice

### Rice Cookers

Where rice is a staple, rice cookers are very much in evidence. You add rice and water, cover, push a button and wait until it's done. Some models have a bell that tells you when the rice is done, which is very convenient. I've tried rice/barley, rice/millet and rice/bean combinations in a cooker, all with great success.

### Stove Top Cooking

Some people prefer to soak rice for an hour or two before cooking, especially in India and Iran. Some people *never* soak rice. I've tried both and find that soaking brown rice gives a *slightly* more tender grain.

### One-Knuckle Rice (no measuring)

Place a quantity of rice in a heavy pot. Jiggle the pot to smooth the surface of the rice. Place an index finger lightly on top of the rice — don't make a dent — and add water until your first knuckle is covered (actually, about 1″ above the rice surface). Remove your finger.

Bring the rice to a boil, cover and simmer on low heat 35 minutes. Turn off heat and let stand, still covered, 10 minutes more.

### Measuring Cup Rice

One part rice to $2\frac{1}{2}$ parts water. Proceed to cook as for One-Knuckle Rice.

**Never add salt** until the rice is done, it toughens the grain, and you probably don't need it.

**Always wash the rice** in several rinses of water to be sure there are no pebbles or hulls.

# Rice Variations

### Barley/Rice
Equal parts rice and barley.
Cook as you would plain rice.
Barley adds a very pleasing silky, almost waxy, texture.

### Millet/Rice
Equal parts rice and millet.
Cook as you would plain rice.
Millet adds a slightly nutty flavour; pleasantly grainy texture.

### Rice with Lentils, Split Peas
Equal parts rice and lentils or peas.
Wash lentils or peas and pick over for stones. Soak 2 hours.
Cook as you would plain rice.
Makes a hearty, rich dish with a rather heavy texture.


## Rice Pilaf (Mid-East)

A savoury pilaf which is especially good with Kebabs.

| | |
|---|---|
| 2 *tablespoons oil* | 1 *cup peeled, seeded and chop-* |
| ½ *cup finely diced green pepper* | *ped tomatoes* |
| ½ *cup finely diced onion* | ½ *pint chicken broth or stock* |
| ½ *cup finely diced celery* | 2 *teaspoons salt* |
| 12 *oz. raw brown rice* | 1 *teaspoon pepper* |
| | ½ *teaspoon oregano* |

1. Heat oil in saucepan. Sauté vegetables until tender. Add rice to mixture, chopped tomatoes and chicken broth and remaining spices.

2. Add just enough water to cover rice. Bring to a gentle boil, decrease heat to low and cover pan. Cook rice until fluffy, about 30 minutes.
   *Serves 4.*

## Jewelled Rice Pilaf (India/Pakistan)

This looks as good as it taste — almost!

2 *tablespoons oil*
$\frac{1}{3}$ *cup chopped onion*
$\frac{1}{4}$ *cup sunflower seeds*
6 *oz. brown rice*
$\frac{1}{3}$ *cup chopped dried apricots*

$\frac{1}{4}$ *cup currants or chopped raisins*
1 *pint boiling water*
*salt and pepper to taste*

Heat the oil in a large pot and sauté the onion until soft. Add the sunflower seeds and rice and cook about 2 minutes more, stirring. Stir in the apricots and currants. Add the boiling water and return to the boil. Cover and simmer 40 minutes or until the rice is done. Season to taste with salt and pepper.
   *Serves 4.*

## Riso Italiano

Something really different to do with leftover rice.

1 *cup cold, cooked brown rice*
2 *tbs. chopped spring onions*
3 *tbs. chopped parsley*
$\frac{1}{2}$ *oz. wheat germ*
3 *anchovies, rinsed with warm water*

2 *cloves garlic, crushed*
2 *tablespoons oil*
1 *tablespoon vinegar\**
2 *teaspoon drained capers (optional)*

\* For this dish, we prefer basil vinegar.

1. Mix together the rice, spring onions, parsley and wheat germ.

2. Mash the anchovies and garlic together. (A mortar and pestle is best for this, but a bowl and spoon will do). Blend in the oil and vinegar.
3. Mix the anchovy mixture with the rice. Toss in the capers.
4. Chill ½ hour before serving.

NOTE: This is very good stuffed into tomato shells.
*Serves 4.*

## Cuban Beans and Rice

From simple ingredients, a great dish.

| | |
|---|---|
| 1 *lb. black (turtle) beans, soaked overnight* | 2 *cloves garlic, chopped* |
| | 1 *teaspoon oregano* |
| 1 *green pepper, chopped* | 1 *bay leaf* |
| 1 *onion, chopped* | |

SOFRITO

| | |
|---|---|
| 1 *onion, chopped* | 1 *teaspoon olive oil* |
| 1 *green pepper, seeded and chopped* | ¼ *cup vinegar* |
| | *salt to taste* |
| 2 *cloves garlic, chopped* | 9 *oz. raw brown rice* |
| 2 *tablespoons vegetable oil* | |

1. Add to the soaked beans 1 green pepper, 1 onion, 2 cloves garlic, and the oregano and bay leaf. Add water to cover by about 1½ inches and cook the beans until done. Add water if needed.
2. Cook the rice.
3. While the rice is cooking, heat the oils and add the *sofrito* onion, pepper and garlic. Cook over moderate heat until the onion is wilted. Add the cooked sofrito and the vinegar to the cooked beans. Add salt to taste.
4. Serve the beans hot, with hot rice to accompany them. Chopped fresh coriander leaves make a nice garnish.

NOTE: This is very good with Salsa Cruda. (See page 121.)
*Serves 4.*

## Khichuri

This dish was the forerunner of our *Kedgeree*. Since the rice and lentils must be soaked 2 hours, then cooked for about 45 minutes, make it a day or two ahead, if you like. It reheats well. Add a little water when reheating, if needed.

### Gujarati Khichuri

| | |
|---|---|
| ¼ *lb. long-grain brown rice* | 1 *medium onion, sliced thin* |
| 2 *oz. lentils* | 1 *clove garlic, sliced thin* |
| 1 *tablespoon oil or ghee* | |

SPICE MIX

| | |
|---|---|
| 1 *teaspoon grated ginger* | ½ *teaspoon cardamom seeds (optional)* |
| ½ *teaspoon turmeric* | |
| ½ *teaspoon cumin seeds* | ¼ *teaspoon cinnamon* |
| ½ *teaspoon freshly ground white pepper* | *pinch cloves* |
| | ¾ *pint boiling water* |

OPTIONAL GARNISHES

| | |
|---|---|
| *salt* | *yogurt* |
| *lemon juice* | *coriander leaves* |

1. Rinse rice and lentils several times, and pick over carefully. Cover with water and soak 2 hours.
2. Drain rice/lentil mixture and spread on linen towel.
3. Heat oil in a heavy pan. Stir in onions and garlic over medium heat until soft but not brown.
4. Stir in spice mix. Stir until fragrance rises.
5. Stir in rice and lentils. Mix thoroughly.
6. Add boiling water. When boiling resumes, cover pot tightly, lower heat and cook over low heat 30 minutes.
7. Let stand, covered, off heat, 10 minutes.
8. Serve hot. Garnish to taste.
   *Serves 4.*

### Bengal Khichuri
Omit spice mixture and omit step 4.
OR limit spices to turmeric and cumin.

## Rajasthan Khichuri
Substitute yellow split peas for lentils.

## Frugal Khichuri
Use cooked rice (about 2 cups)
And cooked lentils (about 1 cup)
All other ingredients (except water) same as **Gujarati Khichuri** or **Bengal Khichuri**
Follow steps 3, 4 and 5 of **Gujarati Khichuri**. Stir to heat rice and lentils thoroughly. If rice is really cold and hard, add about ¼ cup of water, cover the pot and cook over low heat 5 to 10 minutes or until water is absorbed.

## Rice Salad Mediterranée

| | |
|---|---|
| 1 *cup cold cooked brown rice* | 3 *tablespoons chopped parsley* |
| ½ *lb. courgettes, diced finely* | 1 *tablespoon capers (optional)* |
| 1 *tablespoon red onion, minced* | ¼ *cup olive oil with* 1 *clove* |
| 1 *ripe tomato, chopped* | *garlic crushed in it* |
| 1 *small green pepper, diced* | *juice of* ½ *lemon* |

Mix rice with vegetables, parsley and capers. Add oil and toss. Add lemon juice and toss to mix well.
   *Serves 4*

# Vegetables

## Cranberry-Filled Acorn Squash (Americas)

3 acorn squash, halved and    ½ teacup honey
  seeded                     3 tablespoons water
2 cups cranberries

1. Wash and pick over the cranberries. Place them in a large pot together with the honey and water and allow to come slowly to a boil, stirring occasionally. Cook for about 5 minutes or until cranberries are "popping" and sauce is thick. Remove from oven heat and let stand.
2. Meanwhile, heat oven to 375°F. With a fork, gently prick the fleshy side of the cut squash, taking care not to pierce the skin.
3. Place the squash cut side down in a shallow pan and add water to the depth of about ½ inch. Cook squash 25 minutes.
4. Remove from oven (leave the oven on) and turn the squash cut side up.
5. Spoon a portion of the cooked cranberry mixture into each squash. Return to the oven and continue baking about 20 minutes more, or until squash is tender
Serves 6.

## Broccoli Italiano

1 large bunch broccoli        2 cloves garlic, crushed
1 oz. butter                  2 tablespoons chopped parsley
2 tablespoons oil             dash Tabasco (optional)
2 anchovies, well rinsed and  ½ teaspoon lemon juice
  chopped

1. Break broccoli into florets and remove or peel tough stems. Steam broccoli in small amount of salted water until barely tender.
2. Melt the butter with the oil in a large frying pan and add all of the remaining ingredients. Add the broccoli and stir to mix well. Serve hot.
   *Serves 4.*

## Zesty Brussels Sprouts (German)

| | |
|---|---|
| 1 *lb. Brussels sprouts* | $\frac{1}{2}$ *teaspoon caraway seeds* |
| 2 *tablespoons water* | $\frac{1}{4}$ *cup plain yogurt* |
| 3 *tablespoons lemon juice* | 1 *tablespoon grated onion* |

1. Trim stems from sprouts and remove all tough and discoloured leaves.
2. Steam the sprouts with the water, lemon juice and caraway seeds for about 12 minutes or until barely tender. Drain and reserve the liquid and keep the sprouts warm.
3. Add the yogurt and onion to the reserved steaming liquid and mix thoroughly. Toss with the Brussels sprouts. Serve hot.
   *Serves 4.*

## Cauliflower Curry (India/Pakistan)

| | |
|---|---|
| 1 *medium head cauliflower, separated into florets* | $\frac{1}{4}$ *teaspoon cayenne* |
| | $\frac{1}{2}$ *teaspoon salt* |
| 1 *large onion, minced* | 1 *teaspoon* garam masala |
| 8 *fl. oz. stock* | *(p. 145)* |
| $\frac{1}{2}$ *teaspoon turmeric* | 2 *oz. yellow raisins* |

1. RANGETOP: Place all ingredients in a large pot. Cook 35 minutes or until tender.
   PRESSURE COOKER: Place all ingredients in cook-

er, bring to pressure. Cook 4 minutes, reduce pressure quickly.

NOTE: Serve hot or cold, best with a generous topping of yogurt.

*Serves 4.*

## Garam Masala

This spice mixture is used in Indian cooking and the ingredients vary from region to region, as well as from cook to cook. There are a few ready-made *garam masala* mixtures available, but the best is made from freshly ground spices. Store in an airtight container in a cool, dark place. Just a pinch can give a real lift to vegetable dishes.

2 *teaspoons freshly ground or powdered coriander seed*
1 *teaspoon freshly ground or powdered cumin seed*
½ *teaspoon freshly ground white pepper*

½ *teaspoon freshly ground or powdered cloves*
½ *teaspoon freshly ground or powdered cinnamon*
½ *teaspoon powdered ginger*
½ *teaspoon freshly ground cardamom seeds*

## Gratinée of Cauliflower (French)

1 *large cauliflower*
2 *eggs*
¼ *pint skimmed milk*
*salt and pepper to taste*

1 *oz. freshly grated Parmesan cheese*
1 *oz. butter*

1. Heat oven to 450°F.
2. Break cauliflower into florets and steam in a small amount of salted water until barely tender. Drain the cauliflower and mash it coarsely.
3. Whisk together the eggs and milk and mix with the cauliflower. Season to taste.

4. Place mixture in a baking dish which has been lightly buttered. (Individual casseroles are nice.) Sprinkle with the cheese and butter.
5. Bake 20 minutes in 450°F. oven. (Smaller baking dishes may cook more quickly.)

## Chayotes (Mirlitons) Rellenos (Americas)

The chayote, which looks like a lumpy green pear, is actually a squash with a sweet, creamy flavour. In this recipe, it's stuffed with a tangy blue cheese mixture, and baked.

2 *chayotes (mirlitons)*
1 *teaspoon garlic oil (or vegetable oil)*
1 *cup chopped onion*
2½ *cups whole-wheat bread crumbs*

2 *eggs, beaten*
6 *oz. crumbled blue cheese*
2 *teaspoons Dijon-style mustard*
½ *teaspoon prepared horseradish (or to taste)*

1. Halve the chayotes from stem to blossom and steam about 40 minutes, or until tender.
2. Heat the garlic oil and sauté the onion until just translucent. Mix the onion with the bread crumbs. Heat oven to 350°F.
3. Remove the seeds from the chayotes. Remove the pulp and mash it well. Add the mashed pulp to the bread crumb mixture. Stir in the eggs, cheese, mustard and horseradish.
4. Stuff the chayotes with the breadcrumb mixture. Place them, stuffing side up, in an oiled baking dish. Bake at 350°F. for 35 minutes or until lightly browned.
*Serves 4.*

## Corn-Cheese Casserole (Americas)

Quick, easy, delicious and satisfying.

1 *tin cream style corn (17 oz.)*
2 *eggs, lightly beaten*
2 *oz. finely grated sharp Ched-*
   *dar cheese*

2 *tbs. chopped chives or spring*
   *onions*
¼ *teaspoon pepper*
2 *tablespoons wheat germ*

1. Heat oven to 350°F. Butter a shallow 2-pint baking dish.
2. Mix corn with eggs, cheese, chives and pepper. Pour into prepared dish. Sprinkle wheat germ on top.
3. Bake at 350°F. for 25 minutes or until set and slightly puffed and browned.
   *Serves 4.*

## Sicilian Fennel

Fennel has a faintly anise-y flavour and a texture that resembles celery. Here's an unusual way to serve it.

1 *head fennel (about 1 lb.)*
1 *tablespoon olive oil*
½ *oz. butter*
1 *clove garlic*

2 *anchovies, rinsed*
2 *tbs. freshly grated Parmesan*
   *cheese*
*sweet paprika for garnish*

1. Wash and trim the fennel and chop the bulb into 1″ chunks. Steam about 10 minutes or until barely tender.
2. While the fennel is steaming, mash together the oil, butter, garlic and anchovies to make a paste.
3. Drain and purée the fennel in a blender or food processor, adding cooking liquid if needed. Add the oil-butter paste to the purée and simmer in a heavy pan over lowest heat for about 20 minutes to blend the flavours. Sprinkle with the Parmesan. Serve hot, garnished with a dash of paprika.
   *Makes 4 servings.*

## Petits Pois s̀ la Française

1 *lb. small peas (preferably*    1 *sprig parsley*
  *freshly shelled)*          1 *oz. butter*
1 *head cos lettuce*         *pinch of salt*
½ *medium onion*          2 *fl. oz. chicken stock or water*

1. Line a heavy pot with the outer leaves of the lettuce. Tie the remaining heart with string, including the parsley sprig so they will not separate during cooking.
2. Place the peas atop the lettuce leaves and add the heart, onion, butter (in small bits), salt and stock.
3. Bring the pot to a high boil. Cover with a water-filled soup plate. Lower heat and simmer 25 minutes. Remove the onion and lettuce heart. Carefully pour the peas into a serving dish, discarding the lettuce leaves. Serve hot.
*Serves 6.*


## Pomodori Ripieni

Italian Stuffed Tomatoes

6 *large, ripe tomatoes*      1 *clove garlic, squished*
½ *cup fresh whole-wheat bread*    *through a press*
  *crumbs*              2 *egg yolks, lightly beaten*
2 *tablespoons yogurt*     4 *tablespoons grated Parmesan*
1 *tablespoon chopped parsley*  2 *tablespoons wheat germ*
                     ½ *cup olive oil*

1. Heat oven to 375°F.
2. Cut the tomatoes in half horizontally, use only the bottom half. (Save the rest for salads.) Scoop out some of the flesh, leaving the shell intact. Mash the scooped-out flesh and set it aside.
3. Mix the crumbs with the yogurt and mix with the mashed tomato. Mix in the parsley, garlic, yolks, Parmesan and wheat germ.
4. Brush a large baking dish with some of the olive oil.

Stuff the tomato shells with the bread crumb mixture. Place in the dish, stuffed side up. Drizzle the remaining olive oil over the tomatoes. Bake for about 30 minutes or until nicely browned. The tomatoes should keep their shape.
*Makes 6 Servings.*

### Spanakopita (Spinach Feta Pie)

| | |
|---|---|
| 2 cups chopped, cooked, drained spinach | 4 eggs |
| 1 cup chopped onion | $1\frac{1}{2}$–2 cups dry whole wheat bread crumbs |
| 2 tablespoons oil | 2 oz butter |
| 3 spring onions, chopped | 4 fl. oz. oil |
| 6 oz. feta cheese, crumbled | filo dough or strudel leaves – |
| $\frac{1}{2}$ cup chopped parsley | purchase fresh or frozen |
| 2 tablespoons chopped dill weed (leaves only!) | |

Put the spinach into a very large mixing bowl. Sauté the onion in the 2 tablespoons oil until translucent. Add it to the spinach. Add the spring onions, feta cheese, parsley and dill and mix well. Beat the eggs lightly, and add to the spinach mixture. Mix well.

Heat oven to 350°F. Oil two 8″ × 8″ × 2″ baking tins. Melt the butter with the remaining oil.

Place a strudel leaf in the bottom of an oiled pan. Don't worry if the edges lap over the sides. Brush the leaf very lightly with the butter-oil mixture, and sprinkle with crumbs. Fold the overlapping edges in neatly, and add another leaf. Brush and sprinkle. Repeat until you have used six leaves. Top the 6th leaf with half of the spinach mixture. Top with six more leaves. Do not brush or sprinkle the top leaf.

Fill the second tin in the same way. Bake the pies for one hour or until lightly brown and puffy.

Cut into squares or wedges with a sharp knife to serve. Serve hot.
*Serves 12.*

Freeze after baking. Thaw in a low oven and heat thoroughly.

## Chard Gratin (Swiss)

2 *lbs. chard leaves*
2 *tablespoons oil*
½ *medium onion, minced*
½ *cup yogurt cheese or Quark*
2 *eggs, lightly beaten*

1 *oz. grated Parmesan cheese*
2 *tablespoons lemon juice*
⅓ *cup fine, dry whole-wheat*
  *breadcrumbs*

1. Wash the chard leaves and steam them above boiling water 5–7 minutes or until soft. Rinse them under cool water. Shred and squeeze out as much moisture as possible. (Save the squeezed-out liquid and steaming liquid for stock.) Chop very fine.
2. Heat the oil in a frying pan. Add the onion and cook, stirring, until onion is soft. Remove pan from heat.
3. Heat oven to 375°F.
4. Place the cheese in a large bowl. Add the eggs, 3 tablespoons of the Parmesan and the lemon juice. Mix until smooth. Add the chard. Remove the onion from the oil with a slotted spoon and add to the chard mixture.
5. Use the oil to coat a shallow baking dish (or several small, individual ones). Sprinkle with half the breadcrumbs. Place the chard mixture in the dish, smoothing with the back of a spoon.
6. Bake at 375°F. for 40 minutes or until top is browned slightly. Serve hot or cold.

## Swiss Chard Catania

1 *lb. Swiss chard*
½ *cup chicken stock*
2 *tablespoons chopped onion*
2 *cloves garlic, minced*

¼ *teaspoon coarse salt*
½ *teaspoon white peppercorns*
3 *anchovy fillets, rinsed well*
2 *teaspoons lemon juice*

1. Wash chard well. Dice stems into ¼″ pieces. Shred greens.
2. Place chard in a pot with the chicken stock and onion. Bring to a boil, cover and cook over low heat 10 minutes or until just wilted. Set aside.
3. In a mortar, combine the garlic, salt, peppercorns, anchovies and lemon juice. Pound to a coarse paste, adding juice from chard as needed.
4. Pour the garlic mixture over the chard and toss to mix well. Cook over high heat until almost all liquid is absorbed.
   *Serves 4.* Good hot or cold.

## Stuffed Onions (Mid-East)

NOTE: Recipe serves 1 — may be doubled or quadrupled

2 *medium-sized onions*
2 *tablespoons oil*
3 *cloves garlic, chopped (optional)*
½ *cup minced onion (see step 1)*
1 *cup cooked kasha (buckwheat groats)*
2 *tablespoons yogurt*
2 *tablespoons wheat germ*
1 *tablespoon soy sauce*
*dash cayenne*
¼ *pint stock*
*minced chives or parsley for garnish*

1. Cut a thin slice from the bottom of the onions so they will stand firm. With a sharp spoon, scoop out the onion leaving a shell ¼-inch thick. Mince the onion bits that have been scooped out.
2. Drop onion shells into boiling water. Parboil 5 minutes. Drain on a rack, open side down. Heat oven to 350°F.
3. Heat the oil, sauté garlic and chopped onion. When onion is soft, stir in kasha, yogurt, wheat germ, soy sauce and cayenne.

4. Heap kasha mixture into onion shells.
5. Butter a heatproof dish just large enough to hold the onions. Place them in it, stuffing side up. Pour the stock around the onions.
6. Bring to a boil on top of the stove. Place in the oven and bake at 350°F. for 45 minutes, basting two or three times.
7. Remove onions to a serving dish.
8. Boil the sauce remaining in the baking dish over high heat until it is reduced by half. Pour over the onions. Garnish with chives or parsley.

## Festive Red Cabbage (German)

1 *head red cabbage, about 2 lbs.*
2 *tablespoons lemon juice*
1 *medium onion, chopped*
1 *bay leaf*
$\frac{1}{4}$ *pint dry red wine*
1 *tart apple, cored and grated*

1. Core the cabbage and chop coarsely.
2. Place all ingredients in a large, heavy saucepan. Bring to a boil, cover and simmer over low heat 45 minutes stirring occasionally. Add water if needed.
3. Discard bay leaf and serve hot.

## Fresh Tomato Sauce (Italian)

1 *tablespoon oil*
1 *onion, chopped*
1 *medium clove garlic, crushed*
2$\frac{1}{2}$ *lbs. ripe tomatoes, peeled, seeded and chopped*
5 *oz. mushrooms, sliced*
3 *tablespoons fresh, chopped parsley*
1 *tablespoon fresh, chopped oregano*
*juice of* 1 *lemon*
*pinch crushed fennel seed*
*dash cayenne*

Heat oil. Sauté onion and garlic until translucent. Stir in mushrooms until wilted. Add all remaining ingredients and stir. Bring to a boil, lower heat and cook at simmer 10 to 15 minutes, or until thick.

## Pissaladière

A very different tomato tart from the Mediterranean.

*whole-wheat pie crust for one*
   *crust pie*
1 *recipe Fresh Tomato Sauce*
   *(p. 152)*
3 *tablespoons oil*
3 *Spanish onions, sliced*

1½ *oz. grated Parmesan*
½ *teaspoon powdered rosemary*
1 *tin flat anchovies*
   *stoned black olives, sliced into*
   *rings*

1. Heat oven to 375°F. Press dough into the bottom of a square baking dish. Chill.
2. Heat the oil and sauté the onions until translucent. Spread the onions over the crust. Top with the tomato sauce and sprinkle with the cheese and rosemary.
3. Rinse the anchovies in warm water and place them on the pie in a lattice pattern. Place olive rings in the spaces between the anchovies.
4. Bake for 25 minutes, or until the crust is brown.

## Imam Bayildi (Mid-East)

*Imam Bayildi*: roughly translates as "the prime minister fainted," but legend disagrees as to whether it was because this dish is so delectable or because it used so much expensive olive oil. We took out most of the oil, but kept all of the flavour.

4 *medium-sized aubergines*
   *(or 2 large)*
*salted water*
¼ *cup oil, preferably olive*
3 *long medium-sized onions,*
   *halved and sliced*
3 *cloves garlic, minced*

3 *medium-sized tomatoes,*
   *peeled, seeded and chopped*
¼ *cup chopped parsley*
*salt*
*freshly ground white pepper*
3 *tablespoons lemon juice*
4 *fl. oz. water*

1. Cut off aubergine stems. If using long aubergines, cut 1 deep slit lengthwise in each to form a pocket. If using large aubergines, cut in half lengthwise and cut deep slits in the fleshy side.
2. Soak aubergine in salted water 30 minutes, drain, squeeze gently and pat dry with paper towels.
3. Heat oil in a frying pan and stir in onions. Cook over medium heat until limp, then stir in garlic. Remove from heat and stir in the tomatoes, parsley, and salt and pepper to taste.
4. Place aubergine, slit side up, in a large, heavy pan. Spoon onion mixture into the slits, stuffing firmly. Spread remaining onion mixture on top. Sprinkle with the lemon juice. Add water, pouring it down the side of the pot so that the onion mixture is not disturbed.
5. Cover pan and simmer gently 1 hour, or until tender. Add water only if needed.
6. Allow aubergine to cool to room temperature. Serve at room temperature or chilled.
   *Serves 4.*

## Aubergine Stroganoff (Not Quite Russian)

A delicious meatless version.

| | |
|---|---|
| 1 *aubergine (1½ lb.) peeled and cut into strips ¼″ × 2″ × ½″* | 8 *fl. oz. stock* |
| 2 *tablespoons soy sauce* | ½ *teaspoon dry mustard* |
| 1 *tablespoon oil* | 1½ *cups yogurt* |
| 4 *oz. mushrooms, sliced* | 3 *tablespoons arrowroot or cornflour mixed with 6 tablespoons water* |
| 1 *medium onion, sliced* | |

1. Drop aubergine slices in boiling water to cover. Simmer 3 minutes or until soft. Drain. Reserve liquid for stock. Sprinkle the aubergine strips with soy sauce and let cool.
2. Brush a hot frying pan with oil and sauté the aubergine until brown.

3. Cook the mushrooms and onion in the stock until soft. Stir in the dry mustard. Stir in the yogurt. Add the aubergine.
4. As the mixture boils, add the arrowroot mixture, a little at a time, stirring, until thickened. Serve hot over cooked brown rice.
*Serves 4.*

## Aubergine Purée (Mid-East)

Aubergines take on a whole new character in this marvellous purée. Goes well with Lamb-Tomato Stew.

| | |
|---|---|
| 1 *large aubergine, 1 lb.* | 1 *cup yogurt* |
| 1 *tablespoon lemon juice* | 2 *oz. sharp Cheddar cheese,* |
| 2 *tbs. oil* | *grated* |
| 1 *oz. whole-wheat flour* | |

1. Char aubergine skin under a grill or over a gas flame at a low heat until aubergine is soft through OR char quickly and bake at 350°F. until soft (10–15 minutes).
2. Peel away the aubergine skin. Chop the flesh coarsely and sprinkle with the lemon juice. Purée in a blender or food processor. Set aside.
3. Heat the oil. Stir in the flour. Stir in the yogurt. When the mixture boils, stir in the aubergine. Cook over moderate heat, stirring until quite thick. NOTE: At this point, dish may be set aside and reheated.
4. Stir the cheese into the hot aubergine mixture.
*Serves 4.*

## Vegetable and Dried Fruit Curry (India/Pakistan)

This unusual curry takes a little time and trouble, but it's definitely worth it.

6 *fl. oz. second extract coconut milk plus enough water to make ¾ pint liquid*
8 *dried apricots (2 oz.)*
4 *dried figs, halved*
1 *large onion, in chunks*
1 *yam, about 8 oz. sliced*
8 *brussels sprouts*
8 *oz. cauliflower, in small pieces*

2 *red or green pepper, diced*
1 *stalk celery*
½ *teaspoon salt*
6 *fl. oz. first extract coconut milk*
¼ *teaspoon cinnamon*
¼ *teaspoon turmeric*
½ *teaspoon coriander*
½ *teaspoon cumin*
2 *tablespoons lemon juice*

COCONUT MILK*

12 *ozs. dried coconut (un-sweetened)*

*Pour ¾ pint boiling water over the coconut and let stand 5 minutes. Squeeze out the liquid and set aside. This is the first extract. Repeat the process with 8 fl. oz. of boiling water. Save the second extract.*

1. Simmer the dried fruits in the 2nd extract coconut milk and water for 25 minutes. Cover the pan tightly as it cooks.
2. When the fruit is done, add the vegetables and ½ teaspoon salt. Cover and simmer 25 minutes more.
3. Stir in the remaining ingredients and heat, but do not boil.
   *Serves 4.*

* Chicken stock may be used, but the flavour will be different.

## Vegetable Casserole (Mid-East)

The chickpeas make this dish really special.

1 *aubergine, about 1 lb.*
2 *tablespoons vegetable oil*

2 *large onions, chopped*
2 *cups cooked, drained chickpeas*

1½ cups stewed tomatoes,    2 *tbs. lemon juice*
  *drained*                     ½ *teaspoon cinnamon*
3 *tablespoons tomato paste*

1. Slice the aubergine about ¼″ thick and steam, covered, on a rack above boiling water for 20 minutes, or until tender. Let cool.
2. Heat the vegetable oil in a large frying pan. Sauté the onions over moderate heat until softened but not browned. Set aside.
3. Heat oven to 350°F. Oil a baking dish that will hold the aubergine in one layer (more or less).
4. Pave the baking dish with aubergine slices. Spread the cooked onion on top. Add the chickpeas in one layer.
5. In blender or food processor, combine the remaining ingredients. Pour over the chickpeas.
6. Cook at 350°F. for 1 hour.
7. Serve hot or cold. May be reheated. A dollop of plain yogurt makes an excellent garnish.
*Serves 6.*

## Chartreuse of Vegetables (French)

A beautiful design in vegetables, moulded in a bowl and baked makes a very dramatic and delicious presentation.

2 *carrots, in small sticks*    *salt and pepper to taste*
½ *cup broccoli florets*       6 *small cabbage leaves, par-*
½ *cup peas*                      *boiled*
1 *small courgette, sliced*    1½ *oz. butter*
8–10 *asparagus spears (tips*   3 *tablespoons oil*
  *only)*                       1 *clove garlic, crushed*
1 *lb. potatoes, cooked and*
  *mashed (do not peel)*

1. Cook each of the vegetables separately until just *barely* tender. (They will be cooked again.) Drain each and chill.
2. Melt the butter and add the oil and garlic. Chill the mixture until thick.

3. Heat oven to 350°F. Spread about ⅓ of the butter mixture thickly in a large, oven-proof bowl. Arrange the carrots, broccoli, peas, courgettes and asparagus in a decorative pattern, pressing them lightly against the buttered bowl. Cover with a layer of mashed potatoes, sprinkle with salt and pepper to taste, and cover with a layer of cabbage leaves.
4. Add a layer of any vegetables not used in the design and finish with another layer of potatoes, salt and pepper and finally, a layer of cabbage leaves.
5. Heat the remaining butter mixture and pour it over the vegetables.
6. Bake at 350°F. for 30 minutes. Run a knife around the bowl and unmould the vegetables onto a warm plate. Serve immediately.

*Serves 4–6.*

## No-Fat Ratatouille (French)

Ratatouille is usually prepared by sautéing each vegetable separately before combining them. We found that by steaming them all together, the flavour of the dish is maintained, while the effort and calories are cut dramatically.

1 *large onion, sliced*
2 *green peppers, seeded, in ¼″ strips*
2 *cloves garlic, chopped*
4 *tomatoes, peeled, seeded and chopped*
1 *aubergine, quartered and sliced ¼″ thick*
3 *courgettes (about 12 oz.), sliced ¼″ thick*
1 *teaspoon salt*
½ *teaspoon pepper*
*juice of one lemon*
3 *fl. oz. white wine*
4 *tablespoons chopped parsley*

Starting with the onion, layer the ingredients, in order, in a large, heavy pan. Cover and simmer over moderate heat 5 minutes. Reduce heat and allow to steam over low heat 15 minutes more. Remove cover and cook over high heat 5 minutes to reduce liquid.

NOTE: Ratatouille is traditionally made with *lots* of olive oil. If you like, sprinkle a little olive oil over the finished stew, or let each diner add it to taste.
Ratatouille reheats very well.
*Serves 4.*
Ratatouille makes a super crêpe filling.

## Vegetable Couscous (North Africa)

This vegetable medley combines textures and flavours to produce a truly superb dish. Add or subtract vegetables as you wish.

| | |
|---|---|
| 1 *lb. couscous (see glossary)* | 2 *peppers, seeded and diced* |
| 3 *cups cooked chickpeas (save liquid)* | 1 *cinnamon stick* |
| | 1 *teaspoon salt* |
| 12 *oz. peeled, diced pumpkin or winter squash* | $\frac{1}{2}$ *teaspoon pepper* |
| 4 *tomatoes, coarsely diced* | $\frac{1}{4}$ *teaspoon cayenne* |
| 2 *onions, coarsely diced* | $\frac{1}{2}$ *lb. fresh or thawed green peas* |

1. Spread couscous on a large platter. Pour on two cups of boiling water. As soon as the couscous is cool enough to touch, rub it between your palms about 6 inches above the platter until all lumps are removed.
2. In the lower half of a couscous pot (see glossary) place the chickpeas, pumpkin, tomatoes, onion, pepper, cinnamon, salt, pepper and cayenne. Add chickpea liquid and enough water to make 4 pints. Bring to a boil. Place the prepared couscous in the perforated upper pot, cover. Lower heat and simmer 15 minutes.
3. Remove couscous to a large bowl, add 12 fl. oz. of the cooking liquid and mix well. Return the couscous to the perforated upper pot. Add peas to the vegetables. Cover as before and simmer 15 minutes more.
4. Arrange couscous on a large platter, making a deep well in the centre. With a slotted spoon, ladle the vegetables into the well in the couscous. Remove and discard the cinnamon stick. Drizzle the couscous and

vegetables with some cooking liquid. Serve the remaining cooking liquid separately.
*Serves 4–6.*

## Stuffed Savoy Cabbage (French)

This terrific version of stuffed cabbage calls for a dark green, curly-leafed Savoy cabbage to be hollowed out and stuffed with a savoury meat and rice mixture. The cabbage is then reshaped and cooked. It's lovely to serve, even better to eat.

| | |
|---|---|
| 1 *large Savoy cabbage* | ¼ *teaspoon basil* |
| 1 *lb. minced beef* | *salt and pepper to taste* |
| 1 *large onion, chopped* | 2 *tablespoons oil* |
| 1 *clove garlic, crushed* | 2 *large carrots, sliced* |
| 4 *teaspoons tomato paste* | 1 *large onion, sliced* |
| ½ *cup cooked brown rice* | 1¼ *pints meat stock (water may* |
| 1 *egg* | *be used)* |
| ½ *teaspoon thyme* | |

1. Drop the whole cabbage into boiling salted water to cover for 10 to 15 minutes.
2. Drain and rinse with cold water. Allow to cool. Remove very tough or discoloured outer leaves.
3. Place cabbage stem side down on a large square of cheesecloth. Gently pry the leaves apart and cut out the core, leaving the stem intact.
4. Mix together the meat, minced onion, garlic, tomato paste, rice, egg, thyme, basil, salt and pepper. Place the mixture into the hollow cabbage and gently reshape the leaves, re-forming the cabbage. Tie the cheesecloth around the cabbage firmly.
5. Heat the oil in a large pan. Sauté the carrots and sliced onion very briefly and add the cabbage and stock. Cover and cook at simmer for 2½–3 hours. Remove the cheesecloth before serving.
*Serves 6.*

## Lemon-Parsley Sauce (Americas)

| | |
|---|---|
| 2 *tablespoons oil* | *juice of ½ lemon* |
| 1 *oz. whole-wheat flour* | 1 *teaspoon minced lemon peel* |
| 1 *tablespoon tahini* | ½ *cup chopped parsley* |
| 8 *fl. oz. water* | |

Heat oil over medium heat. Stir in the flour and stir for 2–3 minutes, until the flour is cooked but not brown. Gradually stir in the tahini and the water. Stir until the mixture reaches the boil. Simmer for about 5 minutes, or until the sauce is thickened. Add the remaining ingredients and cook for about 2 minutes more. *Serve hot.*

## Walnut-Pecan Ring (Americas)

A delicious vegetarian main dish.

| | |
|---|---|
| 2 *medium stalks celery, finely chopped* | 2 *tablespoons finely chopped parsley* |
| 1 *carrot, finely chopped* | 1 *tablespoon kelp powder or ½ teaspoon salt* |
| ½ *medium onion, finely chopped* | |
| 1½ *cups dry whole-grain bread or cracker crumbs* | 2 *tablespoons soy sauce* |
| 6 *oz. walnuts, ground coarsely* | 1½ *cups plain yogurt* |
| 6 *oz. pecans, ground coarsely* | 3 *eggs, lightly beaten* |

1. Oil a 3 pint mould. Heat oven to 375°F.
2. Mix together the celery, carrot, onion, crumbs, walnuts, pecans, parsley and kelp.
3. Mix together the soy sauce, yogurt and eggs. Add the soy sauce mixture to the nut mixture and stir very well.
4. Spread into the mould and bake for about one hour, or until the sides of the loaf pull away from the mould.
5. Let cool in the mould for 10 minutes. Loosen with a damp knife. Unmould onto a warm plate. Serve with lemon-parsley sauce (page     ).
*Serves 6.*

## Pesto

I admit to a passion for basil, and *pesto* is most definitely a celebration of fresh basil. Although pesto is meant to be used as a sauce for pasta, I add it to soups, stews, salads, or anything else that strikes my fancy. If my basil patch were more abundant, I would use it even more lavishly, but I share the recipe with you in hopes that you will enjoy it, too.

| | |
|---|---|
| 4 *cups tightly packed, washed basil leaves* | 4–6 *cloves chopped garlic* |
| 2 *tbs. chopped parsley* | 2 *oz. pine nuts* |
| 3 *tbs. oil* | 1 *oz. Parmesan cheese, grated* |
| 3 *tbs. olive oil* | *salt to taste* |

Purée all of the above in a blender, pushing the leaves down with a rubber spatula if needed. Place in a jar and refrigerate, covered with a layer of olive oil. Add to sauces, or toss with hot pasta.

## Tahini Dressing (Mid-East)

Serve with hot or cold vegetables, salads or fish.

| | |
|---|---|
| 1 *clove garlic, crushed* | 2 *tablespoons cold water* |
| 2 *tbs. tahini (sesame butter)* | 2 *tablespoons chopped parsley* |
| 2 *tbs. lemon juice* | *or coriander (optional)* |

1. Mix garlic, tahini, lemon juice and water in blender. Add parsley or coriander if desired. Blend thoroughly. *Makes about ½ a cup.*

# Breads & Pastries

### Pioneer Bread

This is an excellent bread, made more nourishing by the addition of lecithin and brewer's yeast. Makes terrific sandwiches.

1 tablespoon active dry yeast
¾ pint warm water (105°–115°F.)
¼ teaspoon powdered ginger
¾ pint water
2 oz. yellow cornmeal
2 tablespoons vegetable oil
½ teacup dark molasses
¼ teacup honey
1 teaspoon salt
14 oz. whole-wheat flour or as needed
½ oz. bran
½ oz. wheat germ
2 tablespoons lecithin powder (optional)
2 oz. brewer's yeast (optional)

1. Sprinkle the active yeast onto the warm water and stir in the ginger. Cover and set aside for about 7 minutes. If the yeast is bubbly, continue the recipe, if not, your yeast is dead and you must begin again.
2. Bring the 2 cups water to a boil. Keeping the water at simmer, sift in the cornmeal by rubbing it between your hands (or sprinkle it in slowly, stirring constantly.) Stir and simmer for 2 minutes. Pour the mixture into the bowl of an electric mixer and stir in the oil, molasses, honey and salt. Cool to 110°F. Add the active yeast, and beat at low speed for 1 minute.
3. Mix the flour together with the bran, wheat germ, lecithin and brewer's yeast. Add 2 cups of this mixture to the cornmeal melange and beat 2–3 minutes more. Using a wooden spoon, stir in another cup or so of the flour mixture, then turn it out onto a floured board and

knead until elastic, adding more of the flour mixture as needed.

4. Lightly grease a large bowl and place the dough in it. Cover with a cloth and set in a warm, draft-free place for about an hour, or until dough has doubled in volume. Smash a fist into the centre of the dough. Turn the dough onto a lightly floured board and let rest for five minutes. Knead briefly to remove air bubbles and form two loaves.

5. Oil two medium (8½ × 4½″) bread tins and place a loaf in each, seam side down. Cover with a cloth and allow to rise in a warm, draft-free place for about 25 minutes.

6. Preheat oven to 350°F. Bake the bread in the centre of the oven for about an hour, or until the bottom crust makes a hollow sound when tapped.

7. Cool on wire racks before slicing.

*Makes two loaves.*

This very dark, very delicious bread freezes well. It has a firm crumb and uniform texture and can be sliced fairly thin.


## Quick Carrot Bread (Americas)

| | |
|---|---|
| ½ *teacup honey* | 1 *teaspoon baking powder* |
| 2 *tbs. molasses* | ½ *teaspoon salt* |
| 4 *fl. oz. oil* | 1 *teaspoon cinnamon* |
| 2 *eggs* | ¼ *teaspoon allspice* |
| ½ *lb. whole wheat flour* | 2 *medium carrots, grated* |
| 1 *teaspoon bicarbonate of soda* | 3 *oz. chopped nuts* |

Beat together the honey, molasses, oil and eggs. Mix the flour, bicarbonate of soda, baking powder, salt, cinnamon and allspice. Blend into the egg mixture. Stir in carrots and nuts. Pour into greased 9″ × 5″ loaf tin. Bake at 350°F. for about 50 minutes, or until bread tests done. Cover baking bread with greaseproof paper after the first 25 minutes of baking to prevent over-browning.

*Makes 1 loaf.*

## Cranberry Bread (Americas)

A wonderful, tart-sweet tea bread.

| | |
|---|---|
| $\frac{1}{2}$ *lb. flour* | 2 *teaspoons grated orange rind* |
| 2 *teaspoons baking powder* | 4 *fl. oz. orange juice* |
| 1 *teaspoon bicarbonate of soda* | 1 *egg* |
| $\frac{1}{2}$ *teaspoon cinnamon* | 1 *cup chopped fresh cranberries* |
| $\frac{1}{8}$ *teaspoon nutmeg* | 2 *oz. sunflower seeds* |
| 2 *oz. butter* | 2 *oz. raisins* |
| $\frac{1}{2}$ *teacup honey* | |

1. Heat oven to 350°F. Oil or grease and flour a 9″ × 5″ loaf tin.
2. Mix together the flour, baking powder, bicarbonate of soda, cinnamon and nutmeg. Cut in the butter until mixture resembles coarse meal.
3. Bake 50 minutes or until done. Cool.
   NOTE: Slices best on the next day.

## Irish Soda Bread

Simple and very good — especially with Irish Stew.

| | |
|---|---|
| 8 *oz. whole-wheat flour* | $\frac{1}{2}$ *teaspoon cream of tartar* |
| 1 *teaspoon salt* | 1 *teaspoon honey* |
| 1 *teaspoon bicarbonate of soda* | $\frac{1}{4}$ *pint buttermilk* |

1. Heat oven to 400°F.
2. Mix the ingredients together in the order given. On a floured board, knead the dough until smooth.
3. Grease a baking sheet.
4. Form a round loaf and place it on the baking sheet. With a razor or very sharp knife, slash an X on the top of the loaf. Be careful not to press down on the dough as you slash.
5. Bake the bread for 40–50 minutes or until brown and crusty.

## English Muffins

¼ *pint water at* 120°F. *with* 1 *teaspoon honey*
1 *oz. active dry yeast*
½ *cup plain yogurt*
¼ *pint boiling water*

12 *oz. whole-wheat flour (approx.)*
1 *teaspoon salt*
½ *teaspoon bicarbonate of soda*
*cornmeal*

1. Dissolve the yeast in the 120°F. water. Cover with a towel and let rest in a warm place 5 minutes. The yeast will be bubbly if it is alive.
2. Mix the yogurt with the boiling water. Stir in the yeast and 8 oz of the flour. Cover and set in a warm place until doubled in bulk, about 45 minutes.
3. Stir in the salt, bicarbonate of soda and remaining flour. Knead until smooth, but rather soft, adding more flour as needed. Form a ball of the dough, replace it in the bowl, cover and let rise again, until doubled, about 30 minutes.
4. Punch the dough down and let rest 10 minutes. Turn onto a floured board and roll ½″ thick. Cut into 3″ rounds (I use a large drinking glass) and dust both sides with cornmeal. Set in a flat pan, cover and let rise until doubled, about 45 minutes. Cook on a girdle or heavy iron frying pan over medium-high heat (about 375°F.) for about 8 minutes on each side. Place on a wire rack and let cool.

To serve, split with a fork and toast lightly.
*Makes a baker's dozen (13).*

## Pumpernickel

1½ *cups vegetable cooking water at* 115°F. *(warm)*
½ *teacup molasses or black treacle*
4 *tablespoons (2 oz.) yeast*

2 *tablespoons vegetable oil*
3 *teaspoons salt*
¾ *lb. rye flour*
2 *oz. gluten flour*
1 *lb. whole wheat flour (about)*

Add the molasses and yeast to the vegetable water, mix, cover and let stand 10 minutes or until the yeast is bubbly.

Add oil and salt to yeast mixture. Mix rye flour, gluten flour, and 2 cups of whole wheat flour. Mix flours into yeast mixture. Add enough wheat flour to make a workable dough.

Turn dough onto a floured board and knead for about 10 minutes. Place dough in oiled bowl, turning to oil all surfaces of the dough. Cover with cloth and set to rise 45 minutes or until doubled in bulk.

Punch dough down. Turn onto a floured board and let rest 10 minutes. While it rests, grease 2 bread pans.

Knead dough 3–4 times. Form 2 loaves. Place loaves in bread pans, seam side down. Cover and set to rise 45 minutes or until doubled. During the last 10 minutes of rise, heat the oven to 450°F.

If you like, carefully brush tops of loaves with melted butter. Bake bread at 450°F. for 10 minutes, reduce heat to 350°F. and bake for 30 minutes more or until done. Remove from pans immediately and cool on wire racks.

## Anisette Toast (Italian)

Great for breakfast! (Make it ahead.)

| | |
|---|---|
| 3 *teaspoons anise seeds* | 1 *teaspoon fresh lemon juice* |
| 2 *eggs, separated* | 4 *oz. whole-wheat flour* |
| ½ *teacup honey* | |

1. Oil an 8″ × 8″ cake tin. Heat oven to 325°F.
2. Crush 2 teaspoons of the anise seed in mortar, until it is a powder.
3. Beat egg whites stiff.
4. Mix yolks with honey, lemon juice, crushed and whole anise seeds. Stir in flour. Fold in egg whites.
5. Spread mixture in prepared tin. Bake for about 20 minutes at 325°F. or until skewer comes out clean.
6. Cool on wire rack. Cut cake in half and cut halves into thinnish slices. Lower heat to 300°F.

7. Place slices on an ungreased baking sheet and toast in the oven for about 15 minutes, turning them over two or three times.
   *About 20 slices.*

## Kulich

Sweet, fruit-filled Russian Easter cake.

8 *fl. oz. milk*
½ *cup honey (at room temperature)*
1 *oz. yeast*
*pinch ginger*
1½ *lbs. whole-wheat flour*
½ *teaspoon salt*
3 *egg yolks*
2 *tablespoons honey*
6 *oz. unsalted butter, melted*
1½ *oz. chopped dried pineapple*

1½ *oz. chopped dried apricots*
3 *oz. whole almonds, toasted and ground*
3 *oz. raisins*
*pinch of saffron, steeped in 2 tbs. boiling water for about 20 minutes*
*crushed seeds from 3 cardamom pods*
1 *teaspoon vanilla*

1. Baking Pans. What you need is two large-capacity tubular shaped tins. If these are unobtainable you may use large cake tins. In either case line them with greaseproof paper which should stand up about three inches above the rim. Fasten this "collar" with a paper clip. Grease the inside of the tin and the collar thoroughly.
2. Scald the milk and cool it to lukewarm (110°F.). Mix the honey with the milk and sprinkle with the yeast and ginger. Let the mixture stand 5–10 minutes until it bubbles. Add the salt and 2 oz of flour and mix well. Cover the bowl and set in a warm place to rise for about 45 minutes.
3. Beat the egg yolks together with the honey until light and stir it into the yeast mixture.
4. Beat the remaining flour and the melted butter into the yeast batter alternately, a little at a time. Beat in the

remaining ingredients. Beat for about 15 minutes more until smooth and elastic.

5. Cover the bowl with a damp cloth and set in a warm place to rise for about 45 minutes or until doubled in bulk. Knead slightly and divide the dough into two parts. Place the dough into the two prepared baking tins. Each tin should be about ½ full. Place a cloth loosely over the tins and set to rise in a warm place until the dough reaches the top of the tins.
6. Meanwhile, heat the oven to 350°F.
7. Bake the kulichi for about 1 hour or until the tops sound hollow when tapped. Turn the kulichi out of the tins and cool them on a wire rack.
8. When cool, the mushroom-shaped tops may be sprinkled with non-instant dry milk to decorate if you like.
9. To serve, cut slices from the bottom or "stem", leaving the top intact as long as possible.

## Stollen (Germany)

A traditional Christmas sweet bread, but an excellent coffeecake, too. Keeps very well.

| | |
|---|---|
| 3 oz. raisins | 1 small container yogurt |
| 3 oz. chopped Honeyed Orange Peel (see p.    ) | ¼ teaspoon salt |
| | 1 egg |
| 4 fl. oz. light rum | ¼ teaspoon almond extract |
| 1 oz. active dry yeast | ¼ teaspoon grated lemon peel |
| 2 fl. oz. water at 115°F. | 3 oz. butter |
| ¼ teacup honey | 6 oz. slivered almonds |
| 12 oz. whole-wheat flour (approx.) | |

1. Have all ingredients at room temperature.
2. Place the raisins and orange peel in a bowl. Pour the rum over them and mix well. Allow to stand at least one hour. Sprinkle the yeast over the water. Mix well. Cover and set aside for 5 minutes or until the yeast is frothy.

3. Drain the fruit, reserving the rum. Sprinkle 1 tablespoon flour over the fruit and mix well.

4. Beat the honey, yogurt, salt, almond extract, lemon peel and reserved rum into the yeast mixture. Place the flour in a large bowl and gradually stir in the yeast mixture. Beat the egg and stir it in. Add 2 oz. butter, a bit at a time, mixing well.

5. Turn the dough onto a floured board and knead until smooth and elastic, adding flour as needed, about 15 minutes. Press in the fruit and almonds.

6. Butter a bowl. Gather the dough into a ball and place in the buttered bowl, turning to coat all sides with butter. Cover with a tea towel and place in a warm spot, free of draughts, for about 1½ hours, or until doubled in bulk. Punch the dough down and let it rest for 10 minutes.

7. Shape the dough into a rectangle about 12″ long and 7″ wide. Brush the surface with ½ ounce melted butter. Fold one long edge of the dough toward the other long edge, stopping about an inch short. Gently pat into place. Taper the ends of the loaf and plump it a bit in the middle. Brush the top of the dough with ¼ oz. melted butter. Place the loaf on a buttered baking sheet, cover with a tea towel and let rise in a warm, draught-free place for 45 minutes, or until doubled in bulk.

8. Bake in the centre of a 350°F. oven for 45 minutes or until brown and crusty. Cool on a wire rack.

## Sour Cream Pastry or Pie Crust

| | |
|---|---|
| 3 *tablespoons sour cream* | ½ *teaspoon salt* |
| 2 *eggs* | ½ *cup oil* |
| 14 *oz. whole-wheat flour* | |

1. Put the sour cream in a small bowl. Add the eggs and beat to mix.

2. Add the salt to the flour and mix. Stir in the oil until the mixture resembles coarse bread crumbs. Stir in the

sour cream-egg mixture. Mix to make a ball of dough. Wrap the ball in waxed paper and refrigerate for at least ½ hour.
*Makes ebough for 2-crust pie.*

## Crêpes

Versatile crêpes can be used to wrap anything from leftover ratatouille to fresh strawberries.

| | |
|---|---|
| 8 *oz. yogurt* | 3 *oz. whole-wheat flour* |
| 3 *eggs* | 2 *fl. oz. water* |

1. Mix all ingredients until smooth and let stand 30 minutes. If batter is too thick, add a little more water. It should have the consistency of heavy cream or buttermilk.
2. Wipe a hot 7″ crêpe pan with oil over moderate heat. Add a scant quarter-cup of batter to the pan and tilt it quickly to cover the bottom with batter. If the batter is too thick, it won't run fast enough. Any "holes" left in the pan can be "patched" with a drop of batter. Cook until the edges appear dry and the batter is set in the centre. Lift the crêpe gently with a spatula and set aside.
3. Repeat until all the batter is used.
   *Makes about 12 crêpes.*
   NOTE: *Wiping* the pan with oil ensures a non-stick surface. Excess oil produces a lacy, fragile crêpe that will fall apart.

   Swirling the batter in the pan takes only a bit of practice. Right-handed beginners might try pouring batter with the left hand while tilting the pan with the right. Lefties do the opposite.

   Crêpes are cooked on one side only.

   Unused crêpes may be frozen in a stack, well-wrapped, with paper between the layers.

# Cakes & Sweets

## Orange Cake (Americas)

I like to bake this moist, flavourful cake in a ring mould or Kugelhapf/Savarin tin.

3 oz. rolled oats
½ pint boiling water
3 oz. butter, melted
1 teacup honey
4 fl. oz. orange juice
1 tablespoon orange zest
2 eggs, lightly beaten

6 oz. whole-wheat flour
3 teaspoons baking powder
½ teaspoon salt
¼ teaspoon cinnamon
¼ teaspoon nutmeg
1 teaspoon vanilla extract

1. Place the rolled oats in a large bowl. Add the boiling water and let stand 20 minutes.
2. Mix together the butter, honey, orange juice and zest, and eggs.
3. Butter and flour a cake pan. Heat oven to 325°F.
4. Stir the egg mixture into the oats.
5. Mix together the flour, baking powder, salt, cinnamon and nutmeg. Add to the oat mixture gradually while stirring. Stir in the vanilla.
6. Smooth the batter into the prepared cake pan. Bake 50 to 55 minutes, or until done. Cool on rack. Dust with powdered milk to garnish.

## Dutch Apple Cake

This cake is not particularly sweet, especially if you prefer tart apples. If you want a sweeter cake, drizzle about 2 tablespoons honey over the cake just before baking.

3 *cups sliced apple (not peeled)*
8 *fl. oz. water*
6 *oz. whole-wheat flour*
1 *tablespoon dry yeast*
2 *tablespoons lecithin (option-*
    *al)*
*dash ginger powder*

2 *tbs. honey*
1 *tablespoon oil*
1 *oz. wheat germ*
1 *egg, lightly beaten*
*cinnamon*
1 *tablespoon lemon juice*

1. All ingredients should be at room temperature. Heat the water to boiling. Place the apple slices on a steamer rack and steam, covered, for 5 minutes. Remove the apples and reserve the steaming liquid.
2. Mix 2 oz of the whole-wheat flour with the yeast, lecithin and ginger. Measure 3 fl. oz. of the apple steaming liquid. Mix with the honey and oil and stir into the flour mixture. Using an electric mixer, beat 2 minutes at medium speed. Beat in the wheat germ and egg. Add the remaining flour gradually until the batter is fairly thick. You may not need all of the flour. Beat at high speed 2 minutes. Spread the batter evenly in a 9″ × 9″ × 2″ tin that has been lightly oiled. Arrange the apple slices on top. Cover with a light cloth and allow to rise in a warm place for about 1 hour or until doubled in bulk.
3. Heat oven to 400°F. Sprinkle the cake with a little cinnamon and the lemon juice. Bake 25 minutes. Cool 10 minutes before removing from pan. Cool on wire rack. Cut into squares.

## Tarte aux Pommes
(French Apple Tart)

CRUST

5 *oz. whole-wheat flour*
1 *egg*

2 *fl. oz. oil*
2 *tablespoons very cold water*

Mix together the egg, oil and water. With a fork, stir in the flour. Knead slightly to make a smooth paste. Wrap and refrigerate 30 minutes.

FILLING

4 *large red-skinned apples* (about 1½ lbs.)
*juice of* 1 *lemon*
¼ *cup honey*
¼ *cup white wine*
4 *oz. curd or cream cheese at room temperature*

1 *tablespoon honey*
1 *tablespoon Cointreau (optional)*
¼ *teaspoon cinnamon (optional)*

1. Core the apples. Slice two of them thinly and toss with 1 tablespoon of the lemon juice. Set aside.
2. Chop the remaining two apples coarsely. Place in a saucepan with the remaining 3 tablespoons lemon juice, honey and white wine. Cook until apples are barely tender. Drain, reserving liquid (there should be about ½ cup.)*
3. Mash the cooked apples (or use a food processor) and mix in the cream cheese, 1 tablespoon honey, Cointreau and cinnamon. Set aside.

TO ASSEMBLE:

1. Butter a tart or cake tin. Heat oven to 400°F.
2. Roll crust between 2 pieces of waxed paper and line the prepared tin. Trim crust neatly.
3. Smooth the apple cheese mixture into the crust. Arrange the sliced apples atop in concentric circles, slightly overlapping.
4. Bake 30 minutes or until lightly browned.
5. While tart is cooling, heat reserved apple-cooking liquid to a boil and cook until reduced by half. Brush over still warm tart — let cool.

*Serves 8.*

* If you do not have ½ cup liquid, add apple juice or cider to make up the difference. Taste, add 1 or 2 teaspoons of honey, if desired.

## Clafoutis

A French cherry pudding.

1 *lb. tart cooking cherries,*
   *stoned\**
¼ *cup brandy (optional)\*\**
2 *oz. whole-wheat flour*
*pinch salt*
3 *tablespoons honey*

3 *eggs, lightly beaten*
8 *fl. oz. milk*
*butter*
*non-instant powdered milk*
   *(optional)*

\* If using tinned cherries, drain.
\*\* If the brandy is omitted, use ⅓ cup apple juice, cherry juice or milk
   in step 3

1. Mix the cherries with brandy and let stand 2–3 hours.
2. Drain cherries. Reserve juice.
1. Mix the flour and salt. Mix 2 tablespoons honey with
   the eggs and stir into the flour. Stir in the milk and
   reserved juice.
4. Butter a shallow baking dish (roughly 10″ × 10″) very
   liberally. Pour in half the batter and cook on top of the
   stove 8–9 minutes or until it begins to set. Use low heat
   and the largest burner you have. Heat oven to 350°F.
5. Spread the cherries evenly over the partly cooked
   batter, top with the remaining batter. Bake at 350°F.
   about 50 minutes or until puffy and lightly browned.
6. The pudding will fall as it cools. It should be served
   warm with a sprinkle of powdered milk (instead of
   icing sugar), or cream.


## Indian Pudding
A great dessert from New England

1½ *pints milk, scalded*
5 *tablespoons cornmeal*
3 *eggs, well beaten*
½ *teacup honey*
½ *cup molasses or black treacle*

1 *teaspoon salt*
½ *teaspoon powdered cinnamon*
½ *teaspoon powdered ginger*
½ *oz. butter (optional)*
*fresh cream or vanilla ice*
   *cream*

Heat oven to 300°F.
   Put cornmeal in a large saucepan. Pour milk over it,

stirring to blend. Bring the mixture slowly to a boil, stirring. Lower the heat to simmer, cook slowly, stirring constantly, until mixture thickens, about 20 minutes.

Mix eggs, honey, treacle, salt, cinnamon and ginger. Stir in the cornmeal mixture. Put mixture into an oiled 5-pint baking dish or casserole and dot with butter, if you like. Bake for about 1 hour or until very thick and brown.

Serve hot, topped with cream or ice cream. As it is very rich, serve *small* portions.

*Serves 6.*

## Pashka

An Eastertime treat from Russia.

| | |
|---|---|
| 3 *lbs. cottage cheese* | 1 *teaspoon vanilla extract* |
| $\frac{1}{2}$ *lb. unsalted butter at room* | 8 *fl. oz. double cream* |
| *temperature* | 4 *egg yolks* |
| 2 *oz. chopped dried pineapple* | $\frac{1}{2}$ *cup honey* |
| 2 *oz. chopped dried apricots* | $\frac{1}{2}$ *cup finely chopped almonds* |

PASHKA MOULD: The Russians use a wooden mould made especially for Pashka. Clean clay flowerpots may be used or two 1-pint plastic cottage cheese containers with holes punched in them from the inside out.

1. Line a colander with cheesecloth and place the cottage cheese in it. Weight with a heavy plate or board and let drain for 2–3 hours.
2. Mix the fruits with the vanilla and let stand for about 1 hour.
3. Rub the drained cottage cheese through a sieve and mix in the butter.
4. Heat the cream to scalding, then remove it from the heat. Whip the egg yolks with the honey until thick and creamy, then beat in the hot cream in a thin stream.
5. Stirring constantly, cook the egg mixture in the top of a double boiler until it is thick and custardy. The mixture will curdle if boiled. Remove from the heat and stir

in the fruit mixture. Stir the custard mixture with a metal spoon, setting the pan in a bowl of ice cubes. Stir until the custard is thoroughly cooled to room temperature. Stir the custard into the cheese mixture and mix in the almonds.

6. Place your Pashka mould in a shallow bowl and line it with damp cheesecloth. The ends of the cheesecloth should hang 2–3 inches outside the mould. Fill the mould (or moulds) with the cheese and cover the top with the ends of the cheesecloth. The cheese must be weighted. We use the plastic lids from cottage cheese or yogurt containers, cut a little smaller than the mould, with a heavy tin on top.

7. Chill the weighted cheese in the refrigerator overnight to drain.

8. The Pashka may be decorated with bits of fruit and almonds.

## Low-Fat Coeurs à la Creme (French)

These delightful confections are meant to be made with cream cheese and double cream. Since we are fond of them, we have invented a lower-calorie, lower-fat version.

| | |
|---|---|
| 8 *oz. curd or cream cheese* | 2 *tablespoons honey* |
| 4 *oz. lowfat cottage cheese* | *dash vanilla extract (optional)* |
| 1 *small container plain yogurt* | |

Blend cheeses with yogurt until smooth. Blend in honey and vanilla. Line Coeurs à la Creme moulds* with damp cheesecloth. Fill with cheese mixture. Cover with damp cheesecloth. Press down firmly. Place moulds on a plate, perforated side down. Refrigerate overnight. Unwrap carefully and serve. Top with a sauce if you like.

* Moulds for Coeurs à la Creme are attractive all by themselves, and are available in most speciality cookware shops. Both porcelain and straw versions are available. As a substitute, you could use almost any basket or a pie tin with perforations in the bottom.

*Makes 4 "hearts".*

## Sunshine Cookies (Americas)

Cookies made with honey instead of sugar aren't crisp, just chewy and marvellous.

4 oz. whole-wheat flour
1 teaspoon baking powder
½ teaspoon salt
½ oz. bran
1 oz. wheat germ
½ teacup oil

¼ teacup honey
2 eggs, lightly beaten
1 teaspoon vanilla
6 oz. raisins
2 oz. sunflower seeds

Mix the flour with the baking powder, salt, bran and wheat germ. Mix together the oil, honey, eggs and vanilla. Stir the egg mixture into the flour mixture. Stir in the raisins and sunflower seeds.

Drop by teaspoonfuls onto an oiled baking sheet. Bake at 350°F. for 10 to 12 minutes. Cook on a wire rack.
*Makes about 4 dozen.*


## Carrot Macaroons (Americas)

Coconuts and carrots add extra sweetness to these yummy macaroons.

2 large grated or shredded carrots
4 fl. oz. oil
¼ teacup honey
1 egg

2 oz. whole-wheat flour
8 oz. grated, flaked or shredded coconut, lightly packed
2 tablespoons lemon juice
1 teaspoon almond flavouring

1. Heat oven to 350°F. Grease 2 or 3 baking sheets. (Recipe makes about 36 two-inch biscuits).
2. Mix ingredients in order given. Drop by teaspoonfuls onto prepared baking sheets. Biscuits are rather free-form and will not spread much during baking.
3. Bake at 300°F. 25 minutes or until browned around edges. Loosen biscuits. Let cool on baking tray.
*Makes about 36 two-inch macaroons.*

## Mango Surprise (Americas)

½ *pint water*      1 *large, ripe mango*
2 *tablespoons agar-agar flakes*    2 *teaspoons lime juice*

1. Place the water in a small saucepan. Add the agar flakes and let stand 10 minutes to soften. Heat just until agar melts, let cool.
2. Peel and dice mango flesh. There should be about 1½ cups. Purée in a blender or food processor.
3. Add the cooled agar mixture to the mango purée. Add the lime juice. Blend or process until smooth.
4. Divide into serving cups. Chill overnight.
   *Serves 4.*

## Rhubarb Sorbet (Mid-East

An unusual refresher.

12 *oz. rhubarb in 2″ chunks*    ½ *pint strawberry kefir (avail-*
¼ *cup water*      *able in natural food stores)*
1 *tablespoon honey*

1. Cook rhubarb, water and honey together for 10 minutes.
2. Purée rhubarb mixture in blender or food processor. Spread in a shallow pan and freeze until firm.
3. Beat the frozen mixture by hand or in a processor until smooth amd mushy. Beat in the kefir.
4. Freeze the mixture until firm.
NOTE: For superior texture, beat the mixture once more and freeze until just firm.

## Honeyed Orange Peel

Use in coffeecakes, American muffins, other confections.

2 *cups shredded peel from un-*    ¾ *cup honey*
   *sprayed, undyed oranges*    *brown rice powder\**

\* Grind long-grain brown rice in a seed or nut mill.

Cover the peels with water. Bring to a boil, boil one minute and drain. Cover with fresh water, boil and drain again. Repeat once more. Pour the honey over the drained peels in a heavy pot. Simmer until the honey is gone. Arrange the peels on an oiled rack and leave in a cool place 8 hours or overnight. Separate the peels if they are sticking together and roll each piece in rice powder, shaking off the excess. Store in a tightly-covered glass container.

*Makes about 1½ cups.*

## Sunny Pumpkin Pie (The Americas)

¼ *pint milk*
¼ *pint cream*
¼ *cup freshly grated orange peel*
3 *whole cloves*
6 *whole allspice*
2 *eggs, lightly beaten*
2 *cups puréed pumpkin or squash*

½ *cup honey*
½ *teaspoon salt*
1 *teaspoon cinnamon*
½ *teaspoon powdered ginger*
1 *ready-to-bake pie shell*

1. Bring the milk and cream to a boil. Remove from the heat, add the orange peel, cloves and allspice and let steep 15 minutes. Strain. Discard the spices.
2. Heat oven to 425°F.
3. Mix together the eggs, pumpkin, honey, salt, cinnamon, ginger, milk and cream. Mix until smooth. Pour into the pie shell.
4. Bake at 425°F. for 15 minutes, then lower heat to 350°F. and bake 50 minutes more or until a knife inserted in the centre of the custard comes out clean. Cool on a rack.

# Pressure Cooking

My grandmothers and mother bottled with pressure cooker bottlers. My mother occasionally cooked a meal in her pressure cooker, but I was raised on the wire whisk/ copper pot school of cooking which regarded pressure cookers with disdain as well as some trepidation. Hasn't everyone heard at least one "exploding cooker" story?

Several years ago, I discovered that pressure cooking has multiple benefits. For one thing, it's a great conserver of energy — both the cook's and the nation's. Quick, high-heat, stove-top cooking uses less fuel than most long-cooking methods. The short cooking time also allows the cook to do something other than watch a pot.

### How it works
Pressure cooking is achieved by sealing a pot then heating the contents, causing expansion and expulsion of air and pressure. The pressure is regulated by the amount of heat applied. A valve on top of the pot allows steam to escape while a regulator on the valve controls the amount released. When a cooker reaches pressure, the regulator begins to rock and hiss. Timing begins *at that moment*. Heat can be reduced, but the regulator should *never* stop rocking until the timing is completed.

### To reduce pressure
When cooking is completed, remove the pan from heat. Pressure will drop naturally and gradually. If a quick drop in pressure is desired, the pan may be immersed halfway in cold water.

### Timing
The important thing to remember when cooking with pressure is that timing is critical. You can't peak, poke or

taste until the cooking is finished and *over*done can't be corrected.

## Steaming

Steamed custards, puddings and breads can be cooked in a pressure cooker if the cooking vessel is set upon a wire rack or trivet. When you select a container for a custard, say, make sure you can easily remove it from your cooker *with hot pads,* for it will be *hot.* We find a straightsided ovenproof glass container the best.

## Buying a cooker

Pressure cookers come in many shapes and sizes. Some have adjustable pressure which is necessary for bottling. Those meant strictly for cooking, however, don't usually have a pressure gauge but reach pressure at a standard 15 pounds. Heavy, stainless steel cookers are the most efficient, safest, and easiest to care for. Our favourite has its sealing mechanism locked from an on-the-lid handle, with two small handles on each side of the pot, making it comfortable to lift and easy to store. Since there is variation among cookers, read the booklet which accompanies yours *carefully* before use.

### Cooking Pulses

Nothing beats pressure cooking for ease and rapidity in cooking beans. *No* more long soaking, *no* more long cooking, with a pressure cooker you can have beans any time at all *without* planning ahead! Here's the **basic method:**

> 1 *cup beans needs:*
> 2 *cups water plus:*
> 1 *tablespoon oil*

1. Place beans, water and oil in cooker. Bring to pressure. Remove cooker from heat and let pressure reduce naturally.
2. Add at least 1 cup water to beans, plus any other desired ingredients. Bring cooker to pressure, cook
   2 *minutes for kidney beans*
   2 *minutes for broad, navy, red, Roman, pink beans*

5 *minutes for black, haricot, pinto beans*
35 *minutes for soybeans* (stubborn!)
Let cooker cool 5 minutes. Reduce pressure quickly.

## Don't Overcrowd

Your cooker needs space, and should never be too full.
Here's how many beans you can cook at one time:
4 pint cooker — ¾ lb. dried beans
8 pint cooker — 1 lb. dried beans
10 pint cooker — 2 lbs. dried beans
12 pint cooker — 3 lbs. dried beans

## Salty Comment

*Don't* add salt until your beans are tender, or they may
remain intractably hard. *Do* be sure to add oil (so they
won't stick). A pinch of savory in the first cooking can help
increase digestibility.

# Glossary

**AGAR AGAR** is derived from seaweed. It is sold by the block (kanten) or as flakes. After being dissolved in boiling liquid, agar-agar turns the cooled liquid to a gel which is firm at room temperature. It is a vegetarian alternative to animal gelatin, but agar contains little protein, only fibre and some minerals. Animal gelatin may be substituted.

**ALCOHOL**. The use of alcohol in cooking dates from antiquity. Wines, spirits and liqueurs are used to flavour many dishes; and since the alcohol cooks away entirely over high heat, the dishes can be ingested with impunity. If you do use alcohol in cooking, use the best; cheap ingredients can't be masked. If you eschew alcohol entirely, substitute a rich stock or an appropriate fruit or vegetable juice. Wine draws calcium from bones into the broth of soups or stews.

**ANNATTO:** Annatto (also called *achiote*) is the seed of a tree native to Central America. The dusky-red seeds impart a subtle flavour to foods, as well as a glorious orange-gold colour. Cheeses are often coloured with annatto. Annatto is available wherever Spanish, South American or Indian/Pakistani products are sold.

TO SOFTEN ANNATTO SEEDS FOR CRUSHING: Cover the seeds with water and bring to a boil. Simmer 5 minutes. Let stand until cool. Drain. Discard water.

**ANNATTO OIL** is bright orange, fragrant and marvellous. You make it by dropping 2 tablespoons *annatto* (also called *achiote*) seeds into 4 tablespoons hot vegetable oil and removing it from the heat. After about 15 minutes, strain and discard the annatto seeds. Use the oil for cooking and store any leftover in the refrigerator. If you don't have annatto oil, just use your usual vegetable oil and proceed with the recipe.

STORE: Annatto seeds keep indefinitely in a tightly covered container away from heat or light.

**ARROWROOT PASTE** is a thickening made from arrowfoot flour and water — 1 part arrowroot to 3 parts water — and is used in exactly the same way as cornflour. Although very similar to cornflour, arrowroot flour is more easily digested. Arrowroot flour is a starch derived from the arrowroot (*Maranta arundinacea*), grown mostly in the West Indies.

**BLACK BEANS** are also called turtle beans. Although the dried beans are black and shiny, when cooked and mashed they appear rich and dark brown. Their flavour is at once hearty and subtle, and quite unique.

**BRAN** is the mostly ingestible outer husk of the wheat kernel. It does contain some vitamins and minerals, but is used for its high fibre content. Relatively tasteless, bran can be added to many dishes, but it absorbs water readily, so it can add an unpleasantly dry "chew" if the liquid portion of a recipe isn't adjusted.

**BULGHUR** is wheat which has been soaked, dried and cracked. Soaked in water for about 30 minutes, it softens to a pleasantly chewy, nutlike grain which can be seasoned and eaten as is, added to cooked dishes, or heated with a little seasoned broth as a side dish. I consider it a staple.

**CHICKPEAS** (*Cicer arietinum*) are also called **ceci** and **garbanzo beans**. In India, where it is a major food crop, the chickpea is known as **Bengal gram**. Originating in western Asia, the chickpea is an important item in the cuisines of the Middle East and Mediterranean.

**CLAY POTS** are ancient cooking utensils enjoying a revival. Foods are placed in a wet clay pot, seasonings added, and the covered pot is placed in a *cold* oven. Foods cook in their own juices, *without added fat*. In addition, the tight-fitting lid keeps in all the nutrients. Clay-pot cooking is not only healthy, but easy (everything goes into the pot at once) and incredibly delicious.

**CORIANDER/CILANTRO**, is also sometimes called Chinese parsley and looks a lot like flat-leaf (Italian) parsley, but its flavour is strong and pungent.

CORIANDER LEAVES are used both as seasoning and flavourful garnish in the cuisines of India, Pakistan, China, Southeast Asia and Mexico. Fresh coriander is widely available and can be kept, refrigerated, for 3 to 5 days, loosely wrapped.

DRIED CORIANDER LEAVES are sometimes available, but I've never found any with even half the flavour of fresh.

CORIANDER SEEDS are more widely used than the leaves, possibly because they are dry and keep indefinitely. They also have a mildly spicy flavour. Seeds are ground and added to foods. Coriander leaves and seeds are *not* interchangeable.

**COUSCOUS** is the name of a dish made from wheat or millet. Cracked millet is favoured in some areas of North Africa where the dish is a staple. The couscous most available in this country is made from seminola wheat and has been pre-cooked, requiring only about 30 minutes of steaming. Read and follow package instructions.

**THE COUSCOUS POT.** Couscous is usually made in a special pot called a couscousière. The lower pot is about 10 inches tall, swelling at the centre to slope inward to the top opening. A second pot with a perforated bottom rests snugly in this opening. This in turn is covered by a flat lid with a few air holes. The stew (vegetables with or without meat) cooks in the lower pot, while the grain (or couscous) steams in the upper pot.

Most couscous pots available in this country are aluminium, and not recommended.

A couscous pot can be fashioned quite easily by placing a colander over a large deep pot. If the fit is loose, twist a tea towel to fill the space between pot and colander.

Nearly any lid will do, as it should allow some steam to escape.

We have a stainless steel "all-purpose-pot" with the same features as a couscousière except that the lid is solid and the sides are straight instead of curved. A spaghetti steamer would probably work as well. There are really only three critical elements:

1. The couscous should *not touch the bubbling stew.*
2. The seal between perforated steamer and stew pot should be tight, forcing the steam up into the couscous.
3. The lid should allow steam to escape.

If the holes in your perforated steamer or colander are too large, line it with a piece of damp cheesecloth or a damp teatowel.

**GARAM MASALA** see page 145

**GARBANZOS** see Chickpeas

**KASHA** is roasted buckwheat groats (hulled grains) which can be cooked into a wonderful side dish (called kasha, too) with a rich, almost smokey taste. Kasha can be purchased whole or cracked. I find the whole grain more satisfying in texture.

**KELP** is dried seaweed and can be used to impart a salty flavour to foods while boosting the mineral content.

**SAFFRON** is the world's most expensive spice. The beautiful, fragrant orange-yellow "threads" of saffron must be picked by hand from a certain species of crocus (*crocus sativus*) and each crocus contains only *three* of these "threads" or styles. It takes about 210,000 crocus styles, hand gleaned, to yield 1 pound. Even so, saffron's unique flavour gives it stature in many of the world's cuisines. Although turmeric can give foods a saffron-like colour, the fragrance and taste of saffron are unmistakable and a little goes a long way.

**SESAME OIL** is a dark, aromatic, flavourful oil extracted from sesame seeds. Since it is rather fragile, it is used sparingly in cooking and is a wonderful garnish for salads and cooked vegetables. Refrigerate.

**SHOYU:** see soy sauce

**SOY SAUCE** needs no introduction, but its inclusion in some unusual recipes may require some explanation. I often use natural soy sauce to colour foods and reduce salt content as a small amount of soy sauce is usually perceived as "saltier" than an equal amount of salt. By using soy sauce or lemon juice, or both, I can reduce the sodium content of recipes while preserving the flavour.

**TAHINI** is a thick, oily paste made by grinding sesame seeds. The oil tends to separate on long standing and requires patient stirring to reconstitute. Available either raw or toasted, tahini has a mild flavour that can be used in both savoury and sweet dishes. Tahini is extremely rich in unprocessed oils and must be kept in the refrigerator to prevent rancidity.

**TURTLE BEANS** see Black Beans.

**YOGURT CHEESE** is just yogurt with some of the liquid removed. To do this, make a bag from 5 or 6 layers of damp cheesecloth, place a quantity of plain yogurt in the bag and hang up to drain for 4–6 hours. The amount of yogurt will be reduced by about $\frac{1}{3}$. Store yogurt cheese, covered tightly, in the refrigerator. Keeps about a week.

**ZEST:** the grated rind of lemon, sometimes orange or lime. Only the outer part of the rind is used, none of the white inner rind.

# Weights and Measures

28 grams = 1 ounce
100 grams = 3½ ounces
454 grams = 1 pound
1 teaspoon = 5 mililitres
1 quart = about 1 litre

1000 micrograms = 1 milligram
1000 MILLIGRAMS = 1 gram
1000 GRAMS = 1 kilogram
.001 grams = 1 milligram
.001 milligram = 1 microgram

$100°F = 38°C$ *warm water*
$180°F = 82°C$ *very hot water*
$250°F = 121°C$ *very slow oven*
$300°F = 149°C$ *slow oven*
$325°F = 163°C$ *slow oven*
$350°F = 177°C$ *moderate oven*
$375°F = 191°C$ *moderate oven*
$400°F = 204°C$ *hot oven*
$425°F = 218°C$ *hot oven*
$450°F = 232°C$ *very hot oven*
To convert °F to °C, subtract
32°, multiply by 5, and divide by 9 $[(°F-32) \times 5 \div 9 = °C]$.

# Index

* Meatless dishes suitable as a main course.

Acorn Squash, Cranberry filled, 143
African Orange Salad, 41
Agar Agar, 184
Alcohol, 184
Anisette Toast, 167
Annatto, 184
  Oil, 184
*Appetizers*
  Avgolemono Sauce, 8
  Baba Ghannouj, 5
  Caponata, 5
  Cherry Syrup for Beverages, 12
  Coquilles St. Jacques, 73
  Dolmades, 7
  Humus bi Tahini, 8
  Liver Paté, 9
  Marvellous Mushroom Paté, 6
  Meatless Dolma*, 128
  Pan Bagna, 10
  Piroshki, 10
  Pitta with Herbs*, 12
  Soufflé Roulade Farcie*, 59
*Apples*
  Dutch Apple Cake, 172
  Tarte aux Pommes, 173
Armenian Lamb Rissoles, 115
Arrowroot Paste, 185
Arroz Con Pollo, 83
Artichoke Soup, Jerusalem, 14
*Aubergines*
  Imam Bayildi*, 153
  Parmigiano*, 62
  Purée, 155
  Stroganoff*, 154
Avgolemono Sauce, 8

Baba Ghannouj, 5
Baccala, Zuppa (soup), 34
Baked Eggs California*, 64
Balkan Christmas Soup, 14
Barbara's Manicotti, 55

Basil – Pesto Sauce, 162
*Beans*
  Black, 185
  Caribbean Soup, 15
  Chili, 119
  Cuban Beans with Rice*, 140
  Fagioli Napolitano, 124
  Felafel Sandwiches*, 126
  Frijoles Negros*, 121
  Meatless Chilli*, 119
  Pressure Cooking, 178
  Russian Salad, 46
  Soybeans Orientale, 126
  Stew with Beef, 97
  Tostadas Compuestas*, 120
*Beef*
  Bean Stew (Mid-East), 97
  Boeuf Bourguignon, 98
  Carbonnades a la Flamande, 100
  Cholent, 96
  Kebabs, marinated, 102
  Keftethes, 116
  Meat and Cherry Stew, 102
  Posole, 101
  Rhubarb Stew, 100
  Rump Steak Rouladen, 95
  Stroganoff, 97
  Yankee Pot Roast, 94
*Beef, Minced*
  Italian Meat Loaf with Sauce, 103
  Picadillo, 104
  Sauce Bolognese, 106
  Swedish Meatballs, 105
  Stuffed Savoy Cabbage, 160

Belgian Chicken Soup, 21
Bengal Gram – see chickpeas
Betty's Menudo, 27
Beverages
  Cherry Syrup, 12
  Gazpacho, 24

* Meatless dishes suitable as a main course.

Black Beans, 185
Boeuf Bourgignon, 98
Bolognese Sauce, 106
Borscht I, 16
    II, 17
Bouillabaise, 18
Bran, 185
*Breads*
    Carrot, 164
    Cranberry, 165
    Irish Soda, 165
    Pioneer, 163
    Pumpernickel, 166
    Quick Carrot, 164
    Stollen, 169
Broccolo Italiano, 143
Brussels Sprouts, Zesty, 144
*Bulghur*, about, 185
    Pilaf, 130
    Tabbouleh Salad, 47

*Cabbage*
    Festive Red, 152
    Piroshki, 10
    Sauerkraut, spareribs with, 99
    Sprout Salad, 45
    Stuffed Savoy, 160
    Rolls, stuffed, 128
Caesar Salad, 37
*Cakes — see also Puddings*
    Dutch Apple, 172
    Kulich, 168
    Orange, 172
Cappriccio, chicken, 76
Caponata, 5
Carbonnades a la Flammande, 100
Caribbean Black Bean Soup, 15
Caribe, Chicken, 76
*Carrot*
    Macaroons, 178
    Quick Bread, 164
    Soup, 19
*Casseroles*
    Corn-Cheese*, 146
    Mid-East Beef Bean Stew, 97
    Moussaka, 114
    Spanish Chicken, 84
    Vegetable*, 156
*Cauliflower*
    Curry, 144
    Gratinée, 145

Ceci — *see chickpeas*
*Chard*
    Gratin, 150
    Lentil Soup, 26
    Swiss Catania, 150
Chartreuse of Vegetables, 157
Chayotes Rellenos, 146
Cheddar Custard*, 58
*Cheese*
    Aubergines Parmigiano*, 62
    Barbara's Manicotti*, 55
    Chard Gratin, 150
    Cheddar Custard*, 58
    Corn Casserole*, 146
    Greek Macaroni Bake*, 57
    Lasagne, 57
    Low Fat Coeurs A La Creme, 177
    Malfatti*, 60
    Pizza Quiche*, 66
    Semi-Classic Quiche*, 65
    Spanakopita*, 149
    Welsh Rarebit*, 61
    Yogurt, 188
*Cherries*
    Clafoutis, 174
    Meat Stew, 102
Cherry Syrup for Beverages, 12
Chestnut Soup, Cream of, 19
*Chicken*
    Abouts
    à la Jerez, 85
    Arroz Con Pollo, 83
    Belgian Soup, 21
    Cappriccio, 76
    Caribe, 76
    Herbed Salad, 42
    Hongroise, 80
    Liz's, 78
    Mexican Marinated, 77
    Molé, 81
    Pakistani Style Barbecued, 87
    Picatta, 89
    Pollo d'Oro, 82
    Potato Salad, 42
    Poulet au Vin Blanc, 80
    Poulet Bordelaise, 78
    Skillet Chicken Italiano, 88
    Spanish Chicken Casserole, 84
    Stock, 35
    with Peaches, 87
    with Pineapple, 86

* Meatless dishes suitable as a main course.

*Chickpeas*, about, 185
  Cakes*, 125
  Humus bi Tahini, 8
  Soup, Herbed, 20
  Stew with Greens, 125
  Vegetable Casserole*, 156
Chicory-Nectarine Salad, 44
Chili Beans, 119
Chili, Meatless*, 119
Cholent, 96
Chowder, see *soups*
Clafoutis, 174
Clay Pots, 185
Coconut Chips, 11
Consomme, see *soups*
Cookies, Sunshine, 178
Coriander, 186
Corn-Cheese Casserole*, 146
*Courgettes*
  Lasagne, 58
*Couscous*, about, 186
  Basic, 116
  Pot, 117
  Vegetable*, 159
Couscousière, 117
Csipetke, 25
*Cranberry*,
  Bread, 165
  Filled Acorn Squash, 143
Crêpes, 171
Cuban Beans with rice*, 140
*Cucumber*
  Raita, 46
  Tomato Salad, 45
  Yogurt Delight, 44
*Curry*
  Cauliflower*, 144
  Lamb, 113
  Lentil with Eggs*, 122
  Vegetable & Dried Fruit*, 156
Custard, Cheddar*, 58

Dolmades, 7
Dolma, Meatless*, 128
Dressings, Salad
  Basic Mustard, 53
  Vinaigrette, 39
Drinks, see *beverages*
*Duck*
  Viennese Duck with Sauerkraut
    Dressing, 90

  with Calico Stuffing, 79
*Dumplings*
  Csipetke, 25
  Malfatti*, 60
Dutch Pea Soup, 29
Dutch Apple Cake, 172

*Eggs*
  Baked California*, 64
  Lentil Curry*, 122
  Omelet Piquante*, 64
  Soufflé Roulade Farcie*, 59
Enchiladas*, 62
English Muffins, 166

Fagioli Napolitano*, 124
Felafel Sandwiches*, 126
Fennel, Sicilian, 147
Festive Red Cabbage, 152
Finochiella, & Pasta*, 134
Fillet of Sole Veronique, 68
*Fish*
  Bouillabaise, 18
  Coquilles St. Jacques, 73
  Fillet of Sole Veronique, 68
  Kulebiaka, 71
  Red Snapper Veracruz, 67
  Scampi, 72
  Souvlakia, 70
  Stock, 36
  Truite au Bleu, 69
  Tuna Sauce for Pasta, 70
  with Tahini Sauce, 69
  Zuppa di Baccala, 34
French Potato Salad, 39
Fruit, Dried & Vegetable Curry*, 156
Fruit Salad Delight, 40
Fried Polenta, 132
Frijoles Negros, 121

Garam Masala, 145, 187
Garbanzos, see *chickpeas*
Gazpacho, 24
Gratinée of Cauliflower, 145
Greek Macaroni Bake*, 57
Greek Salad, 38
Guacamole, 21
Gujarati Khichuri, 141
Gulyas Soup, 24

Herbed Chicken Salad, 42
Herbed Chickpea Soup, 20

* Meatless dishes suitable as a main course.

Herbed Lamb Stew, 110
Herbed Pasta, 134
Homemade Mustard, 51
Hongroise, chicken, 80
Honeyed Orange Peel, 179
Hopi Lamb Stew, 108
Humus Bi Tahini, 8

Imam Bayildi, 153
Indian Lamb on Skewers, 112
Indian Pudding, 175
Irish Soda Bread, 165
Irish Stew, 109
Israeli Fruit Soup, 23
Italian Lentil Soup, 26
Italian Meat Loaf, 103

Jellied Consommé, Citron, 22
Jerusalem Artichoke Soup, 14
Jewelled Rice Pilaf, 139
Juices – *see beverages*

*Kashka*, about, 187
  Basic, 130
  Pilaf, 131
*Kebabs*
  Fish Souvlakia, 70
  Lamb Shashlik, 113
  Marinated Beef, 102
Keftethes (Greek Meatballs), 116
Kelp, 187
Khichuri
  About, 141
  Bengal, 141
  Gujarati, 141
  Rajasthan, 142
Kulebiaka, 71
Kulich, 168

*Lamb*
  Armenian Lamb Rissoles, 115
  Curry, 113
  Herbed Lamb Stew, 110
  Hopi Stew, 108
  Indian, on skewers, 112
  Irish Stew, 109
  Keftethes (Greek Meatballs), 116
  Lemoned Roast, 108
  Marinated Chops, 112
  Meat & Cherry Stew, 102
  Moussaka, 114

Shashlik, 113
Spanish Stew, 110
Tomato Stew, 111
*Lasagne*
  Cheese, 57
  Courgettes*, 58
Lemon-Parsley Sauce, 161
Lemoned Lamb Roast, 108
Lemon Mustard, 53
*Lentils*
  Curry with Eggs*, 122
  Italian Lentil Soup, 26
  Meatless Chili*, 119
  Salad, 47
  Spiced Golden, 123
  with Dried Fruit, 123
  with Chard Soup, 26
Levantine Potato Salad, 43
Liz's Chicken, 78
Liver Paté, 9
Low-Fat Coeurs a la Creme, 177

Macaroni Greek Bake*, 57
Macaroons, Carrot, 178
Malfatti, 60
Mango Surprise, 179
Manicotti Barbara's, 55
Marinated Beef Kebabs, 102
Marinated Lamb Chops, 112
Marvellous Mushroom Pate, 6
Meat & Cherry Stew, 102
Meat Loaf, Italian with Sauce, 103
*Meatballs*
  Kefthethes, 116
  Swedish, 105
Meatless Chili*, 119
Meatless Dolma*, 128
Mexican Christmas Salad, 41
Mexican Marinated Chicken, 77
Mexican Rice Soup, 30
Middle Eastern Beef & Bean Stew, 97
Millet, Steamed, 129
Minestrone, 28
Molé, Chicken, 81
Moussaka, 114
Muffins, English, 166
Mushroom Paté, Marvellous, 6
*Mustard*
  Facts, 49
  Basic Spiced, 51
  Basic Salad Dressing, 53

* Meatless dishes suitable as a main course.

Homemade, 51
Lemon, 53
Prepared, 50
Sauce for Rabbit, 92
Seeds, 49
Sweet-Hot, 52
Tarragon, 52

Nectarine & Chicory Salad, 44
Nicoise, Salade, 38
Noodles, *see also Pasta*
Lasagne, 57
Macaroni, Greek Bake, 57
Nuts
Walnut-Pecan Ring*, 161

*Oils*
Sesame, 187
Tahini, 188
Onion Soup, Parisian Style, 28
Onions, Stuffed, 151
Omelet, Piquante, 64
Orange, Honeyed Peel, 179
Orange Cake, 172
Osso Buco, 106

Pan Bagna, 10
Pakistani Style Barbecue Chicken, 87
Parsley, Lemon sauce with, 161
Pashka, 176
*Pasta*
e Finocchiella, 134
Fagioli Napolitano, with, 124
Herbed, 134
Jardinière, 132
Manicotti, Barbara's, 55
Tarhonya, 132
Paté, Liver, 9
Marvellous Mushroom, 6
*Pastry*
Piroshki, 10
Sour Cream, 170
Peaches, with Chicken, 87
*Peas*
Dutch Pea Soup, 29
Petits Pois à la Française, 148
Pecan Walnut Ring*, 161
Pesto, 162
Picadillo, 104
Picatta, chicken, 89

*Pilaf*
Bulghur, 130
Jewelled Rice, 139
Khichuri, 141
Kasha, 131
Rice, 138
Pineapple, with Chicken, 86
Pioneer Bread, 163
Piroshki, 10
Pissaladière, 153
Pistou, 31
Pitta with Herbs, 12
Pizza Quiche, 66
Polenta, 131
Fried, 132
Pollo D'Oro, 82
Pomodori Rippieni*, 148
*Pork*
Spareribs with Sauerkraut, 99
Posole, 101
*Potatoes*
Chicken Potato Salad, 42
French Potato Salad, 39
Levantine Potato Salad, 43
Poulet au Vin Blanc, 80
Poulet Bordelaise, 78
Pressure Cooking, 181–183
Provençal Farmhouse Soup, 32
*Puddings*
Clafoutis, 174
Indian, 175
Kulich, 168
Low-Fat Coeurs a la Creme, 177
Mango Surprise, 179
Pashka, 176
Rhubarb Sorbet, 179
Sunny Pumpkin Pie, 180
Tarte aux Pommes, 173
Pumpernickel, 166
Pumpkin Pie, 180

Quick Carrot Bread, 164
Quick Corn Chowder, 23
*Quiche*
Pizza*, 66
Semi-Classic*, 65

*Rabbit*
Provençal, 92
with Mustard Sauce, 92
Ratatouille, no fat, 158

* Meatless dishes suitable as a main course.

Red Snapper Veracruz, 67
*Rhubarb*
  Beef Stew, 100
  Sorbet, 179
*Rice*
  How To Cook, 137
  Cuban Beans*, 140
  Facts, 135
  Jewelled Pilaf, 139
  Mexican Soup, 30
  Nutrition, 136
  Pilaf, 138
  Riso Italiano, 139
  Salad Mediterranée, 142
  Variations, 138
Rump Steak Rouladen, 95
Russian Bean Salad, 46

Saffron, 187
Salad Dressings, *see Dressings*
*Salads*
  African Orange, 41
  Cabbage & Sprout, 45
  Caesar, 37
  Chicken Potato, 42
  Chicory-Nectarine, 44
  Cucumber Raita, 46
  Cucumber Yogurt Delight, 44
  French Potato, 39
  Fruit Salad Delight, 40
  Greek, 38
  Herbed Chicken, 42
  Lentil, 47
  Levantine Potato, 43
  Mexican Christmas, 40
  Nicoise, 38
  Pan Bagna, 10
  Rice Salad Mediterranée, 142
  Russian Bean, 46
  Tabbouleh-Bulghur, 47
  Tomato Cucumber, 45
  Waldorf, 41
Salsa Cruda, 121
*Sandwiches*
  Felafel*, 126
  Pitta with Herbs*, 12
*Sauces*
  Avgolemono, 8
  Bolognese, 106
  Enchiladas, 62
  Fresh Tomato, 152

Lemon-Parsley, 161
Molé, 81
Mustard, 92
Napolitano, 124
Pesto, 162
Picadillo, 104
Tahini, 69
Tuna Sauce for Pasta, 70
Sauerkraut Dressing, 90
Sauerkraut, Pork with, 99
Scampi, 72
Scotch Broth, 32
Semi-Classic Quiche, 65
Sesame Oil, 187
Shoyu, *see Soy Sauce*
Sicilian Fennel, 147
Skillet Chicken Italiano, 88
*Snacks*
  Coconut Chips, 11
Soufflé Roulade Farcie, 59
Soupe au Pistou, 31
*Soups*
  Balkan Christmas, 14
  Belgian Chicken, 21
  Betty's Menudo, 27
  Borscht I, 16
  Borscht II, 17
  Bouillabaise, 18
  Caribbean Black Bean, 15
  Carrot, 19
  Chicken Stock, 35
  Chowder, Quick Corn, 23
  Consommé, Jellied Citron, 22
  Cream of Chestnut, 19
  Dutch Pea, 29
  Fish Stock, 36
  Gazpacho, 24
  Gulyas, 24
  Herbed Chick Pea, 20
  Israeli Fruit, 23
  Italian Lentil, 26
  Jellied Consommé Citron, 22
  Jerusalem Artichoke, 14
  Lentil and Chard, 26
  Mexican Rice, 30
  Minestrone, 28
  Onion, Parisian Style, 28
  Provençal Farmhouse, 32
  Quick Corn Chowder, 23
  Scotch Broth, 32
  Soupe au Pistou, 30

* Meatless dishes suitable as a main course.

Stracciatella, 33
Stroganoff, 34
Zuppa di Baccala, 34
Sour Cream Pastry, 170
Souvlakia, 70
Soybeans Orientale, 126
Soy Sauce, 188
Spanakopita*, 149
Spanish Chicken Casserole, 84
Spanish Lamb Stew, 110
Spareribs with Sauerkraut, 99
Spiced Golden Lentils, 123
*Spices*
    Annatto, 184
    Coriander, 186
    Garam Masala, 187
    Saffron, 187
Sprout & Cabbage Salad, 45
Steamed Millet, 129
*Stock*
    Chicken, 35
    Fish, 36
Stollen, 169
Stracciatella, 33
*Stroganoff*
    Aubergines*, 154
    Beef, 97
    Soup, 34
*Stuffed*
    Cabbage Rolls*, 128
    Grape Leaves*, 128
    Dolmades, 7
    Onions, 151
    Savoy Cabbage, 160
    Pomodori Ripieni*, 148
Swedish Meatballs, 105
Sweets, *see Puddings*
Swiss Chard, 150
Sunny Pumpkin Pie, 180
Sunshine Cookies, 178
Syrup, Cherry, 12

Tabbouleh, 47
*Tahini*, 188
    Sauce, 69
Tarhonya, 132
Tarte aux Pommes, 173
Toast, Anisette, 167
*Tomato*
    Cucumber Salad, 45

Fresh Sauce, 152
Lamb Stew, 111
Pissaladière, 153
Pomodori Ripieni*, 148
Tostadas Compuestas*, 120
Trout, 69
Truite au Bleu, 69
Tuna Sauce for Pasta, 70
Turtle Beans, *see Black Beans*,
Turkey Tetrazzini, 90

*Veal*
    Osso Buco, 106
*Vegetable*
    Casserole*, 156
    Chartreuse, 157
    Couscous*, 159
    Dried Fruit Curry*, 156
    Ratatouille, 158
Viennese Duck with Sauerkraut
    Dressing, 90
Vinaigrette, 39

Waldorf Salad, 41
Walnut-Pecan Ring*, 161
Waterzooi, 21
Weights & Measures, 190
Welsh Rarebit, 61
*Whole Grains*
    Bulghur, 185
        Pilaf, 130
        Salad, Tabbouleh, 47
    Jewelled Rice Pilaf, 139
    Khichuri, 141
    Kasha, 187
        Basic, 130
        Pilaf, 131
    Meatless Dolma*, 128
    Steamed Millet, 129

Yankee Pot Roast, 94
*Yogurt*
    Cheese, 188
    Cucumber Delight, 44

Zest, 188
Zesty Brussels Sprouts, 144
Zuppa di Baccala, 34